Anglo-Welsh Wars
1050–1300

Anglo-Welsh Wars
1050–1300

Stuart Ivinson

Wrexham

First published in Wales
in 2001
by
BRIDGE BOOKS
61 Park Avenue
Wrexham
LL12 7AW

ISBN 1-872424-86-4

A CIP entry for this book is available from
the British Library

Printed and bound by
MFP
Manchester

CONTENTS

Maps

Illustrations

ACKNOWLEDGEMENTS

The completion of this work finds me deeply indebted to to a number of people, several of whom require a special mention.

Firstly Professor Anthony Carr of University of Wales, Bangor, my tutor during several great years of study, from which this book ultimately springs.

Secondly Mr Bob Morris, also of the University of Wales, Bangor; his advice and guidance in converting this work from a dissertation to a book was invaluable.

Thirdly, Mr Alister Williams of Bridge Books for seeing the potential in my thesis and for publishing it.

My partner Dawn Phythian deserves a special note, for suggesting that I should seek a publisher in the first place, for being my unofficial secretary and for putting up with me!

Finally, my parents, who have always supported me in my ambitions. I could not have done this without them. Thanks.

Stuart Ivinson, MA
2001

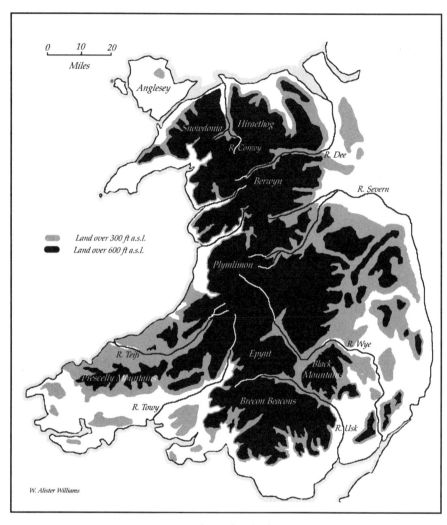

Wales: Physical

INTRODUCTION

Geography has always been a major factor in all aspects of life in Wales. This is as true of warfare as of any other matter, especially in north Wales, a land well suited for defence because of its mountains and rugged terrain. The major geographical features of Wales are the mountain ranges which stretch from Snowdonia and the Berwyns in the north, to the Brecon Beacons and the Black Mountains in the south. During the middle ages these highland areas were blanketed with trees, providing a great deal of natural cover for the inhabitants.

From these highlands rivers flow to all the cardinal points of the compass, and divide Wales into five general areas; the north-west, north-east, central and south-east, and the south-west. Of these areas, the north-west is most heavily defended with mountains, thus rendering invasion more difficult. The relative lack of high ground in the other regions and especially the south has the effect of facilitating invasion, a situation which is rendered worse still by the rivers which flow through these lowlands. Several of these, the Wye to Monmouth, the Monnow to Chepstow, and the Tywi as far as Carmarthen are navigable, and thus act as routes into the heart of the surrounding areas. This topographically inferior terrain was overrun and settled by the Normans only a few years after the invasion of England in 1066.

The north however, after an initial surge of Norman occupation, was able to throw off the yoke and remain largely free of direct foreign intervention until the final conquest of 1282–1283. The men of the north were masters at defending their land, and it was from Gwynedd that the campaigns of the thirteenth century princes were launched. Gwynedd did not owe its status as premiere lordship in Pura Wallia (Native Wales) merely because it was ruled by successive lines of aggressive and dominant princes, but because its natural topography shielded it from all landward attacks, and therefore gave those same dominant princes a great advantage over their less fortunate rivals.

Three concentric rings of highland protected the lords of Gwynedd, with the great bastion of Snowdonia in the centre. These mountain walls were further strengthened as the decades wore on, with the construction of castles at strategic points, Dolforwyn, Dolbadarn, and Carndochan amongst them. Not only did these huge expanses of rugged terrain provide excellent defence, but also supplied their inhabitants with ample pastures for cattle and sheep, and there were no easily navigable rivers penetrating this heart-land. Instead, rivers such as the Conwy and Dee flowed between the hills, effectively flanking them with wide tidal estuaries which required boats to cross them. If an invading army could not cross, then it was faced with a hard march inland seeking for crossings, ascending into the difficult hills and prone to the harrying attacks of defenders upon its flanks. Behind these defences sheltered the island of Anglesey, a fertile arable plain which was a natural granary.

Not only was north Wales a land suited for defence, the same physical features made it an excellent place from which to launch offensives. The mountain shield had the effect of making all attacks from Gwynedd down hill, through easily defended mountain passes, into the lower lying lands of Ceredigion, Powys, and the Perfeddwlad. Natural geography had the effect of shaping the economy, society and political layout of Wales, and the very style of warfare that the Welsh employed both between themselves and against foreign threats.

Chapter 1
The Welsh and the Vikings

It would be wrong to suggest that the tactics employed by the Welsh in defending their homeland were augmented by the land itself. The Welsh were aided by their terrain because they adapted their style of fighting to it. Little is known about the actual mechanics of war in early mediaeval Wales. How forces were raised and victualed, and how they were paid and rewarded for their service is not always clear due to a dearth of information. Much however can be inferred and a picture of how the Welsh defended themselves can be drawn.

Some of the best information about military organisation comes from the laws of Hywel Dda. These laws envisage war as a local and personal thing, between one lord and another. In effect it was seen as little more than an extensive form of cattle raiding. The laws stated that the king of any of the petty kingdoms which made up Wales should receive one third of all booty which came into his realm, and that he could raise taxes to support his warband. This army would be led by the king in person or one of his immediate family. His force would be made up of freemen from his realm, and all freemen over the age of fourteen years were eligible to join if needed. Only freemen were expected to fight; it was both their right and duty to do so. Bondmen were not expected to take part in battle, but they had a role to play. They would assist with the logistics of the army, supplying horses, victuals, equipment and servants to look after it. This was a vital role, for small though these native armies may have been, they still needed to be properly supplied and maintained when on the march, and using non combatants left the fighting arm of the host free to prosecute the campaign. When on the defensive these armies would withdraw to defended sites or caerau, or take to the hills and await the attacking forces, hoping to ambush and disperse them.[1] It has been suggested that a Welsh king may have emplaced free kindred groups in specific parts of his realm, effectively garrisoning strategic locations against attack.[2]

Though this obligation to serve in battle could supply the bulk of a force when needed, the men would not be trained soldiers. In common with all other kingdoms of western Europe at this time, the Welsh kings had a small retinue of picked men to provide a spine for their armies. These men were the teulu, its members were all aristocratic warriors who lived at the kings court and were generously kept by him. In return they owed their lord absolute loyalty and would accompany him on all his journeys. Mounted for mobility their uses were manifold. They owed their lord six weeks of service outside of his own demesne each year, and such campaigns usually took the form of sudden raids of plunder and rapine. Each member of the teulu was entitled to his share of any plunder taken, which in a sense made these retinues partially self sufficient. It seems that other lords could also have their own teulu, a retinue presumably smaller than their king's.

The major Welsh style of warfare was not to engage in pitched battle and static actions, but to fight a war of mobility, launching hit and run raids and fighting sharp, fierce actions. Such rapid assaults would result in either a quick victory or a swift retreat if opposition to the raiding force was too fierce. It was of course a very different style of battle to that pursued by their foreign adversaries, the heavy infantry of the Anglo-Saxons and the armoured Norman knights. Both of these peoples preferred set piece engagements and pitched battles rather than guerilla ambushes, and both peoples suffered at the hands of the Welsh.

The Welsh soldiers were predominantly lightly armoured footmen. They may well have used horses for mobility, but Welsh horses, abundant though they were, were small rangy beasts which did not make good cavalry mounts. Therefore it is likely that warbands would be composed of fast moving and highly mobile mounted infantry, but no true cavalry troopers. Their favoured style of fighting was close quarter, as is reflected in the types of weapons that were employed, swords, knives, spears and longbows of elm wood. These were all close combat weapons, though of course a spear could be thrown as well as used as a pike. The longbows, though powerful enough to pierce mail armour had a fairly short killing range. Thus they would be used only in the opening stages of a fight, or as the attackers emerged from ambush. For defence armour was rare, and the common soldier would satisfy himself with a shield.

A close order cavalry charge or a determined onslaught from heavy infantry would disperse and defeat a ragged warband such as this more often than not if it was caught in the open. In the rough and familiar Welsh terrain however, the natives could often retreat on foot where a more heavily armed horse or footman simply could not follow. In denying an enemy the chance to bring them to open battle the Welsh conserved their own strength as they drained that of the invader, making him march

Uchelwr or Breyer, 10th Century — *literally translated as a 'High Man', an Uchelwr had the status of a nobleman or freeman.*

This warrior is wearing a helmet which, although there is no definite evidence for in Wales, would probably have been worn. Many of the wealthier warriors would have had access to the markets of Chester and Dublin and archaeology shows that items produced as far away as Italy were available to the very wealthy.

Linen trousers, linen and silk tunics and the woollen coat all point to the affluence of this individual. Under the coat (which would probably not have been worn in battle) he wears a suit of mail which gave protection against cutting blows. He is not, however, wearing the padding which was used by many other (foreign) soldiers. Over the mail is a belt from which is suspended a scramasax and a scabbarded double-edged sword.

fruitlessly through hard terrain where they were vulnerable to adverse weather and constant harrying. In this way a small and comparatively ill-equipped Welsh force could waste and ultimately defeat a far larger and better equipped enemy.

The mobile tactics employed by the Welsh were aided by the fact that much of the population lived a transhumance lifestyle, pasturing their herds and flocks in the highlands in the summer and the lowlands in winter. In times of war or in the face of an enemy threat, a population used to such a

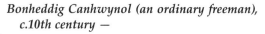

Bonheddig Canhwynol (an ordinary freeman), c.10th century —

the clothing of the ordinary freeman would have consisted of the generic crys (tunic) worn with trousers or breeches and a brychan (cloak). A hood, although not specifically depicted in early medieval Welsh art, was a commonplace item of clothing throughout northern Europe as were leather or sheepskin caps.

This warrior is obviously of a lower class than the Uchelwr (see previous page). He is carrying a spear, a weapon for which the north Welsh were justly famous. On his belt (beneath his brychan) he wears a scramasax, the single-edged knife carried almost universally during this period. His middle-class status is shown more by the colours used in his clothing than by the equipment he carries.

way of life could easily retreat with a minimum of effort, taking their goods, chattels and livestock with them to the safety of high ground and forest strong holds, whilst their lord and his warband defended them. The two campaigns launched by king William Rufus into Wales in 1095 and 1097 ground to an unimpressive halt due to the refusal of the Welsh to stand and give battle to the Norman hosts. In both years the Welsh defenders, 'Sought a defence in their woods and their wildernesses,' and with no enemy to fight and no plunder to be taken Rufus, 'Returned home empty handed and having gained naught.'[3]

Ideally suited to defence and the repulse of larger and better armies as it was, Welsh strategy found little favour amongst commentators of the day.

Gerald of Wales attributed the act of hit and run raiding not to tactical brilliance, but to a lack of knowledge in the arts of war, and indeed plain cowardice'. From their first fierce onslaught they seem most formidable opponents. If the enemy resists manfully and they are repulsed, they are immediately thrown into confusion. With further resistance they turn their backs, seeking safety in flight.'[4] Despite this harsh criticism of Welsh tactical ability, Gerald does admit that his fellow countrymen can be a most irksome enemy to face,

> Although beaten today and shamefully put to flight, tomorrow they march out again, no whit dejected by their defeat or their losses. They may not shine in open combat and in fixed formation, but they harass the enemy by their ambushes and night attacks. In a simple battle they are easily beaten, but they are difficult to conquer in a long war.[5]

This admiration of their tenacity is only given grudgingly, and it is clear that Gerald did not fully appreciate the tactical excellence of the Welsh mode of war. It was their very willingness to break off an engagement, and their constant harassing of an enemy which made them so hard to defeat in a long war.

However the Welsh did not limit themselves merely to defending their own territory. In the border lands raiding for plunder was a major form of counter attack against Anglo-Saxon or Norman aggression, and when on the offensive in such a manner they often ignored military targets. Towns and villages were frequently raided, as killing civilians and burning crops limited an opponents ability to retaliate. A raid into Shropshire in 1249 for example, burned the settlements of Lydham, Churchstoke, Bromton, Bacheldre and Montgomery, though the castle of Montgomery was left intact, being deemed too difficult a target.[6]

When launching their attacks against foreign invaders or rival Welshmen, the warbands often preferred to use the hours of darkness to cover their manoeuvring and the final assault. The attack upon Hawarden castle in March 1282, the event which sparked the rebellion and final conquest of Wales in that year, was launched at night.

Wales was never free of foreign influence throughout the middle ages. As the Welsh fought along the shifting border with the Anglo-Saxon kingdoms, both sides fell under the influence of the Viking raiders from Scandinavia. Though evidence of Scandinavian settlement is sparse, the Vikings had a profound impact upon Wales and the Welsh. The first recorded raid upon Wales was made in 850 when one Cyngen was killed by them.[7] Three years later the first raid was made upon Anglesey, which was to become a prime target for the Vikings. The religious houses of Caer Gybi and Ynys Seiriol lay surrounded by rich and fertile arable land, and all were raided frequently in the years following 853. The 'Sunday battle' fought in 876 took place on Anglesey, in which the forces of Rhodri Mawr king of Gwynedd (844–878) were defeated by a Viking host. The raiders had come from Ireland where the Scandinavian enclaves, especially the kingdom of Dublin, were used as staging posts for raids throughout the Irish Sea region. Many other parts of Wales suffered raids, the coastal regions of the south and east and especially St. David's monastery. Brycheiniog, Gwent and Gwynllwg were attacked by Vikings from England in 896.[8]

The advent of the Vikings in England and later in Wales led to political alliances between kings in efforts to defeat the Scandinavian threat. In the tenth century Hywel Dda consolidated much of Wales under his power and allied himself with the court of Wessex against the Vikings before his death in 950.

The Vikings did not just bring devastation and sacrilege to Wales. These hardy warriors from Dublin soon came to be seen as a source of mercenaries to use against both Anglo-Saxons and Welshmen. The extra strength a band of Viking warriors provided a Welsh host could often be invaluable to a king who could keep them under control. Unfortunately they often proved to be unruly allies, and a king who lost control of his Viking hirelings frequently had to face the very devastation he was trying to avoid as they ran amok. Even their conversion to Christianity during the eleventh century did not sate the Scandinavian appetite for rapine, and monasteries continued to be a prime target. In 1080 St. David's was once again sacked and bishop Abraham was murdered.[9] Nevertheless Viking mercenaries came to be used extensively by many Welsh kings in their internecine and intercerstine wars. During the civil war in Gwynedd between Hywel ap Ieuaf and his uncle Iago, Vikings in Hywel's employ sacked the church of Clynnog Fawr in 978, and a year later captured Iago, handing him over to Hywel who then ascended the throne.

The impact the Vikings had both as mercenaries and as raiders politically was enormous. Indeed, there is a body of evidence which suggests that north Wales was in fact held in overlordship by the Vikings during the early eleventh century. Brut y Tywysogyon (The Chronicle of the Princes) states that in 989, 'Maredudd ab Owain gave a penny from every person as a tribute to the Black host.'[10] More evidence is provided by the History of Gruffydd ap Cynan, which states that one Olaf of Dublin ruled a realm which included the Isle of Man, Galloway, Anglesey and Gwynedd.

Furthermore, after the battle of Clontarf in 1014 the victorious Irish over-kings began to claim that they now held the right of overlordship over Wales as well. The sheer scale of Viking activity in north Wales from the mid tenth to the mid eleventh centuries would suggest an overlordship of some kind, ended by the rising might of Gruffudd ap Llywelyn, which rendered overlordship from Dublin obsolete.[11]

Brut Y Tywysogyon states that Hywel's mercenaries who sacked Clynnog Fawr in 978 were Saxons. This may be a mistake or it could show that Hywel had extensive mercenary forces made up of both Vikings and Saxons.[12] Such tripartite alliances were not uncommon.

In 1055 Gruffudd ap Llywelyn of Gwynedd allied with the exiled Earl Aelfgar of Mercia, and the two recruited a Viking host in Ireland to uphold the Mercian's cause. They invaded Hereford, ruled by king Edward the Confessor's Norman favourite Earl Ralph of Mantes and heavily defeated him in battle. The earl had experimented by mounting his English troops in the Norman fashion, but it was a disaster. Earl Harold of Wessex led an unsuccessful counter offensive into Wales, and the truce of that year saw Aelfgar restored to Mercia, and Gruffudd ap Llywelyn swore to be a client king under Edward. The following year Gruffudd and his Vikings raided into Herefordshire, withdrawing and submitting once more to King Edward when Harold again threatened him with an army. Two years later in 1058, Aelfgar was again outlawed and again turned to Ireland and Gruffudd to restore him. Once more Viking mercenaries under Aelfgar and Gruffudd marched into England and restored him.

Such were the political alliances that grew up between the Welsh and the Vikings that Dublin came to be used as a place of refuge in times of need. One such refugee was Cynan ab Iago, whose father had been deposed from the throne of Gwynedd by Gruffudd ap Llywelyn in 1039. Whilst in Dublin, Cynan married King Olaf's daughter and his half Viking son Gruffudd sought aid to regain Gwynedd following Gruffudd ap Llywelyn's death in 1063–1064. In 1073 he attacked with a mercenary fleet but was defeated in 1075 at the battle of Bron-yr-erw and returned to Ireland. Further efforts to regain Gwynedd were made, including a campaign of 1081 which culminated in the battle of Mynydd Carn, which again saw the heavy use of Vikings.

Gruffudd seized power in 1094 but was defeated four years later by a Norman army under the earls of Chester and Shrewsbury. As the Normans ravaged Anglesey they were heavily defeated by a Viking fleet, and in the fighting earl Hugh of Shrewsbury was shot and killed by an arrow in the eye. In one of history's small ironies the man who reputedly killed him was the fleet's leader King Magnus Barefoot of Norway, the son of King Harold Hardrada who had died at Stamford Bridge in 1066.

Whether this meeting was a full scale battle is unknown. The Saga of Magnus Barefoot implies that it may have been, but is unclear: 'When he came to the sound of Anglesey there came against him an army from Wales, which was led by two earls. They began immediately to give battle, and there was a severe conflict.'[13] The History of Gruffudd ap Cynan is more ambiguous. It states that the Normans,

> Advanced towards the King and his guard of three ships. The king and his followers fought against them valiantly, and the French fell dead from their horses like fruit from their branches, some dead, some wounded by the missiles of the Norsemen. The King himself rising up in the prow of the boat, wounded in the eye with an arrow Hugh Earl of Shrewsbury, and he fell mortally wounded to the earth from his armoured horse.[14]

Hugh's death occurred as the Vikings drew towards the shore, but whether they disembarked cannot be inferred.

Gruffudd ap Cynan then assumed the throne of Gwynedd and was this time able to keep it. He and his Vikings had stopped the Norman onslaught against north Wales. It must have been apparent to the Normans by this time that any advances they made in Gwynedd would always be susceptible to counter attacks from Dublin, and therefore any control they had over north Wales would be tenuous.

Gruffudd ap Cynan's sons Cadwaladr and Owain Gwynedd also made use of Vikings in their campaigns. The last recorded incident of Viking activity in Wales was in 1144 when Cadwaladr enlisted their aid in a feud with his brother. The Norman assault upon Ireland from 1169 onwards though finally halted the flow of Vikings into Welsh affairs. Welsh lords could no longer rely upon Vikings to make up their armies, and could no longer retreat from danger to refuge in Dublin, which now became a crown lordship.

At no point throughout the middle ages until the conquest in 1282, was the situation a simple one of Englishman against Welshman. Cross border alliances abounded, as the example of Gruffudd ap Llywelyn and Earl Aelfgar shows. The Welsh would often enlist the aid of Marcher lords, and More often, perhaps, the Marchers would enlist Welshmen. The end result was the same: a local and temporary alliance of Marcher and Welsh lords against a common enemy, be he Welsh or Marcher himself. For example in 1067 the brothers Bleddyn and Rhiwallon, kings of Gwynedd and Powys respectively aided Eadric the Wild in an attack upon Herefordshire. In 1085

Aillt, c.10th century —

a term used during the early medieval period to describe both the free and unfree clients of a lord, similar to an English subject or villain.

This figure is wearing the longer style of linen crys (tunic) which is dyed blue. This immediately places him within a specific socio-economic group as blue was quite an expensive colour to produce. He is carrying a longbow, which was the chosen weapon of many south Welsh warriors. His arrows are carried in a leather quiver suspended from his belt. Many medieval manuscripts depict Welsh archers with only one shoe, the other foot being bare. To date, there has been no explanation for this.

the Norman invasion of Llyn had help from the Welsh of Powys. Royal campaigns too could often rely on Welsh support. King John's campaign of 1211 was assisted by Welshmen and even Edward I's of 1277 was stoutly aided by Welshmen disaffected with Llywelyn ap Gruffudd.

Despite Gerald of Wales' damning indictment of the Welsh's ability in warfare, it is apparent that they were a tactically astute people, well aware of how to defend their kingdoms from foreign threats. That more and more of Wales was gradually annexed as the period progressed does not detract from this. The fact that they were not engulfed in a single rush, as England, a larger, united and more powerful kingdom was in 1066, demonstrates their military ability. The Welsh knew what had to be done to defend their kingdoms, and generally they were successful. They would ally for the moment with whatever forces gave them the best chance of success, Viking, Anglo Saxon, Norman lord or English king. Just as readily they would turn upon them when the alliance had served its usefulness. Such activity earned them a reputation for perfidiousness, but it was merely intelligent. Though great tracts of Wales fell to the Normans, much of it was often regained in the successful counter attacks of the thirteenth century, and never was all of Wales subjugated until 1282, over two hundred years after England fell to the Normans after one major battle and a handfull of short campaigns.

Thus we can believe with justification that the Welsh were adept at the art of war, and, having reviewed their abilities, we must now turn our attention to those of their adversaries.

Notes

1. D. Nicolle, *Arthur and the Anglo-Saxon wars*, London, Osprey, 1995, p.16.
2. G. R. J. Jones, 'The defences of Gwynedd in the thirteenth century', *Transactions of the Caernarvonshire Historical Society*, 1969, vol.XXX, pp.40–41.
3. Brut y Tywysogion, pp.19-20.
4. Gerald of Wales, *The description of Wales*, p.259.
5. Gerald of Wales, *The description of Wales*, p.260.
6. F. Suppe, *Military institutions on the Welsh Marches*, Suffolk, Woodbridge, 1994, pp.9–11.
7. Brut y Tywysogion, p.5.
8. Brut y Tywysogion, p.5.
9. Brut y Tywysogion, p.17.
10. Brut y Tywysogion, p.10.

11. W. Davies, *Patterns of power in early Wales*, Oxford, Oxford University Press, 1990, pp.52-60.

12. B. G. Charles, *Old Norse relations with Wales*, Cardiff, University of Wales Press, 1934, p.24.

13. S. Laing, *Snorri Sturluson*, Heimskringla, London, Everyman, 1951, p.263.

14. A. Jones, *The history of Gruffydd ap Llywelyn*, Manchester, Manchester University Press, 1910, p.147.

Chapter 2
The Anglo-Saxons

By the mid seventh century the Saxon kingdom of Mercia had consolidated its hold on the region of Shropshire and Herefordshire. Expansion ceased at this point, as stiffening Welsh resistance made it clear to the Saxons that conquest of the uplands which now faced them would come at a high cost. Thus King Offa established a border with the Welsh delineating it with Offa's Dyke. In efforts to stabilise the border, Mercian kings frequently led campaigns and raids into Wales; in 769, 816, 818 and 822 for example. This pressure on Wales only slackened when the power of Mercia began to decline.[1]

Hence there was a long history of warfare between Wales and the Anglo-Saxons, whose numerous kingdoms had by the eleventh century been forged into a single political entity. Under King Edward the Confessor (1042–66) England was sub-divided into several large earldoms, based upon the old kingdoms, ruled over by their earls, of which Earl Harold of Wessex would become foremost. He ultimately succeeded Edward to the crown in 1066. It was to men such as Harold that Edward looked to provide the muscle behind his throne, for by and large it was the earls of England in 1050 who were responsible for the defence of the country.

The kingdom of England was by the eleventh century capable of putting a potent fighting force into the field and had the logistical ability to maintain it for a reasonable period of time. It was the duty of every freeman to defend his home and land if needed. Most of these freemen possessed weapons of their own, as required by law, and were also obliged to build and maintain bridges and defensive works.[2] Every shire in England had its own army, or fyrd, and it was rare that a fyrd ever served outside its own shire.

Though useful to defend their own shire, this large band of men were generally unskilled in the arts of warfare, and thus proved to be an unwieldy and ill equipped force unsuitable for anything else.[3] Certainly a general fyrd such as this was unsuitable to fight an extended or highly mobile campaign against a more professional enemy, and such campaigns became the norm in the tenth and eleventh centuries against the Viking raiders.

The Vikings had a major impact upon English warfare, just as they had upon Welsh. However, in England the Vikings provoked a different response, probably due to the enormous effect Viking settlement had upon England. Although Anglo-Saxon lords undoubtedly used Viking mercenaries and entered into alliances with Viking leaders, the English response to the Viking threat was to adapt their fighting style and institutions to fight them off, rather than to use them and thereby in a sense pay them off. Large, static bands of under-equipped troops were done away with, and the Anglo-Saxons turned to raising smaller forces of more mobile and better equipped warriors. These troops were superior in training to the men of the general fyrds, and were better able to react to a sudden Viking assault. They could pursue and attempt to bring the enemy to battle, rather than sit and wait for them to attack, and hope to beat them off if they did. This shift to a far more aggressive mode of defence, brought with it a change in tactics, and Viking ways and equipment began to filter into Anglo-Saxon armies. Shield walls, coats of mail and Danish battle axes all became more common.

These new Saxon armies were the select fyrds of the shires.[4] It was still the obligation of all freemen to be available to serve in them, but new criteria were introduced to qualify a man for actual service. Connected to land tenure, one man was expected to serve in the shire's select fyrd from given parcels of land. He would be a fully equipped soldier, mounted on horseback for mobility and equipped with shield, helmet and preferably a byrnie (shirt) of mail along with his personal weapons. He would also be fully supplied with the victuals and other equipment he needed for a campaign of up to two months duration, or supplied with a given sum of money to equip himself. It was the duty of all the other freemen of this fyrdsman's unit of land to give him the equipment and money he needed. Every one of these units was effectively self sufficient in supplying and equipping one fully armed soldier for a two month campaign every year. Also, should the need for local defence become critical, the men of the select fyrd would form a semi-professional core of quality soldiers for the greater fyrd to form around.[5]

A most useful source for showing the workings of this system is

Viking Hersir, c.*9th/10th C —*
this man's equipment suggests
that he is a nobleman or veteran
warrior. His spangenhelm
(helmet) is of a type similar to one
found at Gjermundbu in Norway,
of late 9th C. date, though with its
cheekpieces, spectacle visor and
rawhide neck guard, it is similar to
the 6th century Swedish vendel and
valsgarde types. His armour is completed with
a mail byrnie, under which is worn a fine
woollen tunic. His breeches are of linen and
the plaid weave suggests a possible Celtic
influence.
He is armed with a high-quality broad-
sword and axe. The lateer, with its acid
etched tracery and runic inscriptions, would
have been very expensive. His shield is made of
wood, trimmed with leather.
Though a Viking, the appearance of this warrior
is similar to that of a Saxon thegn of the period.

Domesday Book. The entry for Berkshire during the time of the Confessor's reign states that,

> If the king sent an army anywhere, only one soldier went from five hides, and four shillings were given to him from each hide as subsistence and wages for two months. This money, indeed, was not sent to the king but was given to the soldiers.[6]

It seems that in Berkshire at any rate, and quite possibly across all of Saxon England, the land unit expected to provide one soldier was five hides. In the areas of England which had been the Danelaw, land was parceled out not in hides but in carucates, and one soldier was supported by six of these. Should

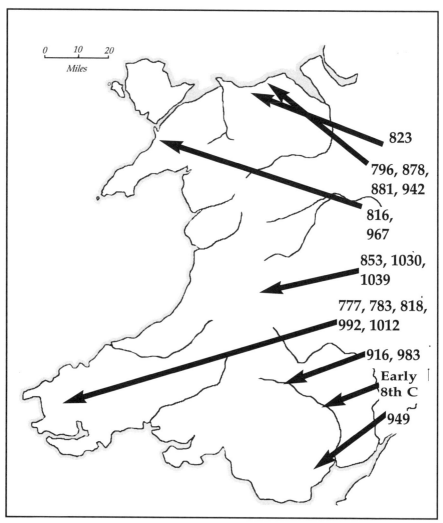

0   10   20
Miles

823

796, 878,
881, 942

816,
967

853, 1030,
1039

777, 783, 818,
992, 1012

916, 983

Early
8th C

949

Wales: English attacks 8th–11th centuries

the service need to be extended beyond the initial two month period, then the king was bound to pay the soldiers from the proceeds of the Danegeld tax.

The evidence would also suggest that the select fyrd system was aimed at recruiting land owners to its ranks, not just commoners. This is suggested by several factors. Firstly each fyrdsman was expected to have a riding horse, and horses of riding quality tended to be expensive beasts. Secondly the quality armour and equipment each man was expected to possess did not come cheap, and finally the level of wages he was to be paid. Four shillings per hide from five hides gives a figure of twenty shillings, ten for each month on campaign service. Though this sum was to be used to supply as well as pay the soldier, it was still an extremely good rate of pay, not dissimilar in fact to that of knights in the post-conquest Norman army.

That select fyrd service was targeted at thegns is further evidenced through a system of fines and penalties, fyrdwite, imposed on those who failed to do service. During the reign of king Ethelred (978–1016) these fines stood at 120 shillings for a thegn and thirty for a commoner. To desert from a royal host cost the miscreant his life and his weregild, and all his lands were taken by the crown. Desertion from an ordinary fyrd cost 120 shillings and possible forfeiture of land.[7] It would seem then that service in the select fyrd was based not just upon land tenure, but also upon lordship. A freeman holding part of a five hide or six carucate unit, was expected either to serve or to contribute a share towards the upkeep of the man who did. A thegn holding a full five hides or more, was expected to appear in person or risk losing his lands. Failure to defend his lordship denied a thegn the right to own that lordship.[8] Many towns also served as five hide units for select fyrd service. Malmesbury and Exeter for example were each assessed as five hides. Others, such as Barnstaple, Lidford and Totnes were grouped together to serve as a single unit of five hides.

Targeted at the thegnage, membership of the select fyrds would not lie exclusively with the nobility, for the simple fact that there would not be enough of them to fill a shire quota of troops. A thegn who held ten hides of his own and had no other thegn as a sub tenant, for example, would have to provide a common freeman instead. Again the Berkshire Domesday survey illustrates this point. In 1086 Berkshire was quoted as having a total population of some 6,324 people, and pre-conquest it had been divided up into 2,502 hides, leading to a select fyrd quota of some 500 men. In 1086 the total number of tenants in chief and under tenants was listed at 265. It is true that many of Berkshire's thegns would have perished in the battles of 1066, but the Conqueror had replaced them with new Norman nobles, so that it is likely that the number of nobles in the shire was probably similar in 1086 to 1066. Therefore, if there were some 260 nobles in Berkshire, there would need to be nearly as many commoners doing service to supply the full quota.[9]

The armies fielded by the eleventh century Anglo-Saxon monarchs were a mixture of thegns and freemen serving for two months and equipped to an adequately high standard. The emphasis on the use of horses for mobility and partial self-sufficiency for supplies meant that they could campaign over large areas without putting too much strain upon the land over which they passed. Nor would they have to disperse to find adequate provisions and were therefore able to maintain their strength which a dispersed force inevitably lost. The same factors generally applied to the organisation of the navy at this time. Every 300 hides across England was meant to supply one ship with a complement of 60 marines equipped with mail byrnies, helmets, shields, swords and axes.

The obligation to serve in the greater fyrd did not cease with the institution of the select fyrd. Of little value on a long or active campaign, the greater fyrd could still be called up for local defensive actions against an imminent threat, and by 1050 can be seen in effect as a home guard. It has been contested whether the greater fyrd ever existed at all, and that throughout the Anglo-Saxon period armies were composed of a lord and his retainers along with select warbands.[10] Certainly the distinction between greater and lesser fyrds was never made by the Anglo-Saxons themselves, but whether we should go as far as to argue that the greater fyrd never existed is certainly debatable. What does seem to be true is that by the second half of the eleventh century the greater fyrd as a fighting force was obsolete.

A typical dark-age helmet of a type known as a spangenhelm. It could equally have been worn by Viking, Anglo-Saxon or Welsh wariors. Its design ultimately harks back to 4th century late-Roman types. It is decorated in a typically Nordic style.

Fyrds, select and greater were organised by shire not just for the purpose of raising the troops, but also to marshal them on the battle field, each shire acting as a unit under its own sub commander. For example in 1010 the Ealdorman Ulfkytel of East Anglia commanded both his own fyrd and that of Cambridgeshire against a Viking host. His own troops broke and fled the field, whilst the men of Cambridgeshire fought on.[11] The great earldoms of men such as Harold of Wessex, Edwin of Mercia and Morcar of Northumbria were made up of several shires each, and naturally their fyrds would also be grouped together under each earl.

The select fyrd could be relied upon to form the bulk of any Anglo-Saxon army. The core of the army had always been the retainers of the king or earl who commanded it. Following Cnut of Denmark's seizure of the throne in 1016 this retinue was transformed into the housecarls. They became the elite of any late Anglo-Saxon army, heavily armed and armoured semi-professional soldiers drawn from the thegnage. They served their lord, were kept by him and rewarded for their service in coin, and less commonly with lands. Payment was not an inducement to serve, but rather a reward for the service they gave, which was based upon bonds of loyalty and lordship. It is clear that when Cnut inaugurated the housecarls in 1016 or soon after, he was creating a highly prestigious unit, its ranks filled only by the high born and the brave. The housecarls were equipped with a double edged sword of high quality, a mail byrnie, helmet, shield, spear and Danish battle axe. They also had to own at least one horse each. The total number of royal housecarls may have numbered around 3000, and they were the best troops in the kingdom, although they did not serve in the king's retinue merely as warriors. During peacetime their roles were varied, ranging from royal tax collectors to ministers of state and witnesses of charters, recipients of land grants and givers of the same.

Earls Harold and Tostig are both noted as having housecarls of their own, and we can assume that all the earls would have housecarls in their retinue. Though courtiers and not just warriors, the housecarls are known best as the front line of the shield wall, the vanguard of the Anglo-Saxon hosts. Just how these hosts were ever brought to the battle field is a matter of some speculation. A select fyrd led by its earl and his housecarls, or the king and his, would be called out to service if a given locality was threatened by enemy action. For a larger and more critical engagement several fyrds would join together, collected from the line of march as the army advanced. Thus we could imagine messengers speeding north from London in 1066, calling the earls and their retinues to service as the royal army under King Harold advanced to York to intercept King Harold of Norway. In such a way

Anglo-Saxon housecarl, late 11th C. —
[© Regia Anglorum]
This man is equipped to a high standard and carries a Dane
axe, the trademark weapon of the later Anglo-Saxons.
His helmet is raised from a single piece of metal, rather
than segmented like the spengenhelm types, and he
wears a heavily padded jacket under his mail
byrnie. Slung across his back is a long tailed kite
shield.

the fyrds could be raised and ready to join with the army as it marched through.

How the army fought once contact with the enemy was made is better known. The major tactic of the Anglo-Saxons was that of the heavy infantry, in disciplined formation fronted by a shield wall. That such a tactic was standard can be inferred from the accounts of the battles of Brunanburh and Maldon, and is also evident at Hastings.

Such a formation could be difficult to break and afforded each soldier a good deal of protection. A shield wall could also stand against mounted men. The Norman knights at Hastings spent most of the day trying to break the Anglo-Saxon line, all the while in danger from the blows of the Danish axes. Ultimately the Normans succeeded, but it can be argued that they faced a severely weakened English army, deprived of many of its best men and comprised of the inexperienced and the weary following the action at Stamford Bridge only a short while before.

One question concerning Anglo-Saxon tactics was whether or not they possessed cavalry. War horses needed to be bigger and stronger that common riding horses, and would cost more to purchase and maintain. Certainly the king and his wealthier magnates would have been able to afford stables of such beasts with which to equip their house-hold troops, and evidence from wills shows that stud farms had existed from the end of the tenth century. However there is little evidence to suggest that the English had cavalry. The only source which mentions cavalry being used is the Heimskringla of Snorri Sturluson, in which he describes the Anglo-Saxons falling upon the Vikings at Stamford Bridge:

For although the English rode against the Northmen, they gave way again immediately, as they could do nothing against them. Now when the Northmen thought they perceived that the enemy were making but weak assaults, they set after them, and would drive them into flight; but when they had broken their shield rampart the Englishmen rode up from all sides, and threw arrows and spears on them.[12]

However this account was written in the thirteenth century and is therefore by no means contemporary, the detail could easily have become confused between the eleventh and the thirteenth centuries. In fact this account sounds very similar to the events of the battle of Hastings, and Snorri might have been confused.

There is a great deal more evidence to suggest that the English did not have cavalry. The equipment of the housecarls, the military elite, suggests that they were not cavalry. That they rode to battle is not in doubt, but neither is the fact that the Danish axe most certainly was not a cavalry weapon.

The only time there is real evidence of the Anglo-Saxons fighting from horseback is shown in the chronicle account of the battle of Brunanburh — 'The whole day long the West Saxons with mounted companies kept in pursuit of the hostile peoples, grievously they cut down the fugitives from behind with their whetted swords.'[13] This is clearly an account of the pursuit of a fleeing enemy, it would seem reasonable to expect the housecarls and fyrdsmen to remain mounted in the pursuit. There is a great deal of difference between soldiers remaining on horse back to chase the enemy away, and the use of genuine cavalry tactics.[14] Perhaps the most telling argument against there being Anglo-Saxon cavalry is the absence of such troops at Hastings. King Harold had been to Normandy and was aware of the use of cavalry, and must have been apprehensive about having to face them. Had he possessed cavalry of his own, even if they were few, surely he would have wanted them with him to face the Normans.

That the five hide system was workable for the raising of troops is clearly demonstrated, but it was not the only system. The Anglo-Saxon Chronicle in 1008 states that Ethelred ordered one battle ship to be built from every 310 hides, not 300, and that every eight hides was to supply a helmet and byrnie.[15] Whether this meant just the equipment, or a man to fill it is unclear, nor is it clear whether this was an additional burden on top of the normal recruitment to produce extra troops in a time of need. It certainly shows that the demands for warriors did not always follow the rule of one from every five hides. Even so, to have any form of partially standard national recruitment was a testament to the organisational abilities of the Anglo-Saxon kings.[16]

It is obvious that relations with Wales were frequently hostile. The king may have been at peace with one kingdom in Wales, but rarely would be so with all of them, so border raiding was never likely to cease completely. Therefore border warfare was endemic to the extent that, 'Domesday Book reveals a ribbon of wasteland in 1066 that stretched along the border from Cheshire to Gloucestershire, an Offa's Dyke of destruction.'[17]The result of this was that military obligation in the border areas of England fell far more heavily than upon any other part of the kingdom. All the burgesses of Hereford were liable for fifteen days of service on campaign if the sheriff called them, as many times a year as was necessary. Failure to attend incurred the fine of forty shillings payable to the king. The only other town in all England where military service was so extensive was Shrewsbury. Furthermore, the freemen of Archenfield were similarly bound to do service, forming the vanguard of an army advancing into Wales, and the rearguard of a retiring one, the local knowledge of the men of the border was highly thought of on campaign. Such an obligation did not go unrewarded, as the men of Archenfield, 'Do not pay tax nor other customary dues, except that they march in the king's army if they have been ordered.'[18]

Obligations were put to the test on numerous occasions following 1050 by Gruffudd ap Llywelyn. He seized power in Gwynedd in 1039 and from 1055 until his death in 1063/4 had all of Wales under his overlordship. It was his border raiding which created the afore-mentioned 'Offa's Dyke' of destruction. During 1055 Earl Aelfgar of Mercia was outlawed. He fled to Ireland to recruit a fleet and together with his son in law, Gruffudd, attacked and destroyed Hereford. Later that year both bishop Leofgar and Aelfnoth, sheriff of Herefordshire were killed in battle. The following year Gruffudd struck again, routing the Anglo-Norman force of Earl Ralph of Hereford. Harold of Wessex mounted an unsuccessful counter-attack and in 1056 Aelfgar was reinstated to Mercia, and Gruffudd 'Swore oaths that he would be a loyal and faithful underking to King Edward.'[19] A second outlawry and offensive ended in the same way in 1058, but when in 1062 Aelfgar died, the king and the earl of Wessex did not hesitate to act.

The sources vary about the date of the campaign, whether it began in 1062 or 1063, but the results were the same.[20] A mounted force rode swiftly from Gloucester to Rhuddlan intent on capturing Gruffudd. He escaped, but Rhuddlan and Gruffudds' fleet was burned and in May 1063 or 1064 Harold commanded a dual campaign against the whole of Wales. He led a ravaging force by sea whilst his brother Tostig commanded the land force which pushed into Gwynedd. This campaign demonstrated that Harold knew how to defeat the Welsh and had adapted the Anglo-Saxon army to do so. He attempted few set piece battles which he knew the Welsh would avoid, instead pursuing them into their strongholds with light troops, launching savage raids in the Welsh fashion. His seaborne troops could flank and cut off the Welsh, and stood to guard against intervention from Dublin. Gruffudd himself may have fled to Dublin at the time of the offensive, but wherever he was, it was a Welshman who killed him, and his head was presented to Harold and then to the king as a sign of victory.

It was a stunning success and testimony to Harold's generalship and the ability of his troops. An English royal campaign in Wales did not achieve similar results again for a long time. Edward installed Gruffudd's half brothers Bleddyn and Rhiwallon ap Cynfyn to Gwynedd and Powys respectively, whereupon they swore oaths to him as their overlord.[21] In Deheubarth a further two new rulers emerged, Maredudd and Rhys ab Owain, and in Morgannwg Cadwgan ap Meurig came to power. Wales had fallen apart once more, such was the success of Harold Godwinson's campaign.

Harold's defeat of the Welsh was to have important repercussions on Welsh history. Had the victorious Normans come against Wales under Gruffudd ap Llywelyn, later events may have gone very differently indeed. The Welsh attitude was summed up neatly by the Brut y Tywysogyon entry for 1066:

> A certain man called William the Bastard, leader of the Normans, and with him a mighty host, came against him [Harold Godwinson]; and after a mighty battle and a slaughter of the Saxons, he despoiled him of his kingdom and of his life, and he defended for himself the kingdom of the Saxons with victorious hand and a mighty noble host.[22]

In the light of the events of 1063 it is not surprising the Welsh were pleased at Harold's death, with him gone they could look to better times. How wrong they were to be proven, when that 'Mighty noble' host turned its attention to the west.

Notes

1. L. H. Nelson, *The Normans in South Wales 1070–1171*, Austin, University of Texas Press, 1966, pp.14–15.
2. D. Nicolle, *Arthur and the Anglo-Saxon wars*, London, Osprey, 1995, p.29.
3. C. W. Hollister, *Anglo-Saxon military institutions*, Oxford, Oxford University Press, 1962, p.27.
4. C. W. Hollister, *Anglo-Saxon military institutions*, Oxford, Oxford University Press, 1962, p.26.
5. C. W. Hollister, *Anglo-Saxon military institutions*, Oxford, Oxford University Press, 1962, pp.30–31.
6. C. W. Hollister, *Anglo-Saxon military institutions*,1962, p.38.
7. H. R. Loyn, *The governance of Anglo-Saxon England*, 1984, pp.163–4.
8. *English Historical Documents*, II Cnut c.77 and c.77.1, p.430.
9. C. W. Hollister, *Anglo-Saxon military institutions*, 1962, pp.80–1.
10. R. P. Abels, *Lordship and military obligation in Anglo-Saxon England*, 1988, pp.175–9.
11. *Anglo-Saxon chronicle*, p.90.
12. S. Laing, (ed.) *Snorri Sturluson. Heimskringla*, London, Everyman, 1951, p.231.
13. *Anglo-Saxon chronicle*, p.69.
14. N. Hooper, 'The Anglo-Saxons at war', in S. C. Hawkes, (ed.) *Weapons and warfare in Anglo-Saxon England*, 1989, pp.199–200.
15. *Anglo-Saxon chronicle*, p.88.
16. R. P. Abels, *Lordship and military obligation in Anglo-Saxon England*, 1988, p.111.
17. R. P Abels, *Lordship and military obligation in Anglo-Saxon England*, 1988, p.171.
18. R. P Abels, *Lordship and military obligation in Anglo-Saxon England*, 1988, p.173.
19. *Anglo-Saxon chronicle*, pp.132–3.
20. B. T. Hudson, 'The destruction of Gruffydd ap Llywelyn', *Welsh History Review*, 1990–1991, pp.331–350.
21. *Anglo-Saxon chronicle*, pp.136–7.
22. *Brut y Tywysogion*, p.15.

Chapter 3
The Normans

The Normans first appeared on the Welsh border in 1051 when the nephew of King Edward the Confessor, Ralph of Mantes, was installed by the king as earl of Hereford. He brought with him to the region a considerable following of fellow Normans and Frenchmen. The new earl soon found himself dragged into the endemic border warfare when, in 1052 Gruffudd ap Llywelyn led a raiding force towards Leominster. Ralph and his force defeated the Welsh and turned them back, but Gruffudd soon returned, in 1055. He led another assault over the border, towards Hereford itself. Earl Ralph again led his forces to meet the enemy, experimenting by mounting his Anglo-Saxons and using them as cavalry in the Norman style, rather than as mounted infantry. This experiment proved to be a terrible disaster and the Anglo-Norman force was routed and smashed. On the strength of this performance, it seemed that the Welsh had little to fear from these foreign favourites of the Confessor, and were not unduly disturbed by their presence.

Far more damaging than this Norman effort was the campaign led by Earls Harold and Tostig in 1063–1064. It left Wales politically fragmented once more, with several minor kings ruling the Welsh whereas there had been one powerful overlord. This was the position in 1066 when Duke William of Normandy conquered England, and his followers promptly turned their attention to the west. The successors of Gruffudd ap Llywelyn had little chance of keeping the Normans out, squabbling amongst themselves as they were. Had Gruffudd still lived, then the course of events may have been different.

To all of the native kingdoms in Britain in 1066 the Normans were something new. Their style of warfare was different in many respects to that of either the Anglo-Saxons or the Welsh. Though the Normans fought pitched battles as the Anglo-Saxons did, the elite of their army was cavalry rather than infantry. The development of such tactics by the Normans was due largely to where they had come from. Much open country lay in northern France, and such terrain is good for horses. Only a small step was needed to make the transition from mounted infantry to cavalry in such an environment. The Franks themselves had a long tradition of mounted fighting and the Normans would have needed little encouragement to adopt their tactics as they settled in France. In Britain, though, this was a new and disturbing phenomenon, for neither Anglo-Saxon nor Welsh armies used cavalry, and in suitable terrain the armoured shock of the Norman horsemen could be unstoppable.

These knights (or *miles*) all bore similar equipment. They were armoured with a knee length mail hauberk which also covered their arms to the elbows. Underneath would be worn a quilted undergarment or gambeson to provide padding. A mail coif was worn underneath a conical helmet fitted with a nasal. To augment the protection afforded by all this armour each knight also carried a large kite shaped shield, often with a curved face, which covered his entire side and leg as he sat on his horse.[1]

The principle offensive item each knight carried was a double-edged

Norman miles, c.1070 —
wearing a mail hauberk and a helmet and armed with a sword lance and kite shaped shield. Mounted soldiers such as this were not ideal for use in the rugged mountain terrain of Wales and were better suited to the coastal lowlands.

sword. Axes and maces were also used, as was the lance. These lances were light and relatively short weapons, no different from a footman's spear. By and large they were used in the old Roman fashion, held approximately half way along the length and wielded with an over-arm stabbing motion. They could also be thrown like javelins, and both techniques are clearly shown on the Bayeux Tapestry. A third technique was also used, the true mediaeval style of couching the lance under-arm in order to deliver the full momentum of the charging horse at the point of impact. A single knight is shown using this technique on the Tapestry, suggesting that it was at this time just being experimentally introduced.[2]

These men were the elite of a Norman army, the smashing power which would be unleashed to destroy an enemy force. Alone however it could be severely limited, and Norman armies did not rely entirely on their cavalry, as is seen at the battle of Hastings. Infantry were as important to the Normans as cavalry, and they came in two general types, heavy foot and archers. The heavy infantry were similarly equipped to the knights, although maybe not to quite the same standard, whereas the archers seem to have carried few accoutrements. Lightly armoured and nimble, the archers used short bows which were probably not as powerful as those of the Welsh, but nevertheless provided vital missile support.[3] When all three arms were used in conjunction, as in the final relentless attacks at Hastings, the result was devastating.

The Anglo-Saxons, with a solid infantry tradition, had much to offer their new masters following 1066, and the question arises as to whether the Normans retained and used the fyrd. Fyrd, a Saxon word, never appears in the post-conquest Latin sources. The chronicler Ordericus Vitalis does mention the use of Angli, or Englishmen by the Norman kings in campaigns in 1068 against the rebellious town of Exeter, 1073 and 1078 fighting on the continent, and in 1075, 1088 and 1101 defending the crown against rebellion and invasion.[4] It is not inconceivable that these Angli were fyrdsmen, and this hypothesis is given credence by two passages in Domesday Book. In 1086 four freemen held between them ten hides of the bishop of Worcester's estate at Bishampton, and owed exactly the same service on land and sea as in 1066 under the fyrd system. Similarly, the town of Bedford was assessed in 1086 as fifty hides for service, just as in 1066. In 1094, according to the Anglo-Saxon chronicle, William II demanded that 20,000 English troops be raised to serve in France, but when they were assembled ten shillings was taken from each man and they were discharged.[5] Ten shillings was of course one month's wages for a fyrdsman, and it would seem that at least until the dawn of the twelfth century the fyrd continued to exist and to be used.

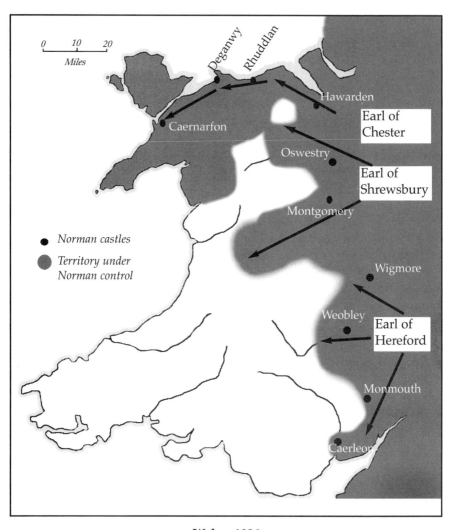

Wales: 1086

The continuance of the fyrd suggests that the post-conquest kingdom of England had a dual military obligation placed upon it. The fyrd was used to provide infantry whilst the cavalry were drawn from the feudal host. The Norman knight owed personal service based upon land tenure. The terms of this service changed considerably throughout the middle ages, but the obligation was established immediately following the conquest by William I. The Ely chronicle of the mid-twelfth century states that in 1088 William II summoned knights according to the quotas his father had laid down. Ordericus Vitalis claimed that William I distributed lands to his followers in return for service, so that 60,000 knights would be available. This figure is wildly exaggerated, but there is no reason to doubt the system it illustrates.[6] Charters of Henry I state that the quota of Evesham's estates, some 160 hides in all, was a mere five knights. William I summoned five men from here in 1072, and they must have been knights, for had it been a fyrd summons then 160 hides could be expected to yield some thirty two men. This therefore would suggest that the quota of knights from the Evesham estates was fixed by 1072.[7] Further evidence to suggest that the entire system of quotas was instigated at one time by a single figure is afforded by the Carta Baronum and the Pipe rolls of Henry II. In these documents, the majority of all quotas represent a figure which is divisible by five, and this uniformity suggests a single instigator.

Anglo-Norman armies were formed of a mixture of troops and troop types. Cavalry and infantry, feudal knights and fyrd infantry all rubbed shoulders on campaign, and were joined by hefty contingents of mercenaries. These mercenaries, usually from Flanders, were considered every bit as trustworthy, often more so, as the levied troops. Mercenary forces had a great deal of flexibility. They would serve for as long as they were contracted to do so, rather than for a short period of time like levied forces. Mercenaries were professional soldiers and their use by the Norman kings increased as time went on. Ultimately mercenaries came to completely replace the fyrdmen in Anglo-Norman armies, the obligation of the fyrd to serve being commuted to cash payments and taxes, which would be used to hire professionals. An early example of this development is given by William II's actions in 1094.

Important though these mercenaries were, the core of Anglo-Norman armies remained the king's own household knights. Several men of note rose to high status through the familia regis, William de Warenne became a member of William I's household before the conquest and served him for the rest of his life thereafter. Warenne was greatly trusted, and by 1086 was the fourth greatest lay magnate in England. He also served William II, being

Norman heavy infantry, late 11th C. —
*The equipment carried by the heavy infantry was no different to that
of the knights. Indeed, as his spurs suggest, this man is a miles
waiting to advance on foot.*
*The neck and chin defence is formed by a padded square
of mail attached to the chest of the hauberk, which laces
to the leather coif on either side of the head. The long
kite shield was developed to protect a horesman's
vulnerable legs but, of course, also proved useful in
infantry formations.*

granted four manors in Surrey in 1088. Warenne's son, also called William, served Henry I faithfully, commanding divisions of the armies at Tinchebrai in 1106 and Bremule in 1119.[8] Household members enjoyed the king's confidence and served him as councillors, and as judges in his courts. They stood at the centre of power, and were not just valued warriors. Robert Beaumont fought at Hastings and Tinchebrai, but was also a chief councillor of William II and a stalwart of Henry I, aiding him in securing his throne. He eventually became earl of Leicester in 1107. These few examples more than adequately show that even at an early stage, the familia regis was a vitally important institution. Its members served as councillors, generals and garrison commanders across the Norman empire. For minor actions or specific tasks the familia regis provided an adequate force of professional knights, which could be expanded upon and used as the command structure and vanguard of a larger army whenever necessary.

It was not long after the battle of Hastings that the Normans first made contact with the Welsh. In 1067 William fitz Osbern was made earl of Hereford, and one of his first actions was to construct several castles upon his new territory; Chepstow, Wigmore and Clifford, the latter two with boroughs, amongst them. Two further border earldoms were created, at Shrewsbury, entrusted to Roger de Montgomery, and Chester, given first to Gherbod the Fleming and then to Hugh of Avranches in 1070. All three earls were borderers from Normandy well versed in border warfare and defence. It was their job to halt the Welsh incursions into England and to restore to prosperity the strip of wasteland which was the result of Gruffudd ap Llywelyn's raiding. Constructing castles and boroughs was but the first stage. Caus, Oswestry and Chirbury became front line positions and were fortified by Earl Roger, who constructed another castle deep into the border zone at Hen Domen. It was used as an advance base for Roger's incursions into Welsh territory. Early incursions from Oswestry pushed into Cynllaith, Edeirnion, Nanheudwy, and Iâl. Ceri, Cydewain and Arwystli were all raided from Hen Domen.

The dominant figure on the border at this time was fitz Osbern, and his influence was considerable. He garrisoned his castles by offering attractive rewards to knights in his service, and many flocked to his banner as a result. Settlers were attracted into the wasteland by the construction of boroughs with considerable privileges. At no point though did he attempt to alienate Welshmen living in his territory. He did not try to displace them, and many settlements were left with their own leaders in place, frequently having any privileges they possessed confirmed.

Thus William fitz Osbern had a considerable influence on the border districts, but his reign in Hereford was cut short. He departed for Normandy in 1070 and a year later was killed in battle. His second son received all his English possessions, but Roger was not the same man his father had been. In 1075 he rebelled against William I because royal officials were interfering in his affairs in Herefordshire. He saw this as an infringement of his rights, but his rebellion was short-lived. He was defeated and imprisoned the same year. Following his defeat the earldom was in abeyance until 1125, and the absence of a powerful leader on the southern border weakened the Norman position and slowed their incursions.

There was of course interaction between the Normans and the Welsh all along the border. The first instance of direct Norman intervention in Welsh affairs came in 1071, when Caradog ap Gruffudd of Gwynllwg enlisted the support of Roger de Montgomery against his enemy Maredudd ab Owain in battle along the river Rhymney. This was but the first instance of Welsh and Norman allying against a common enemy. Gruffudd ap Cynan had the aid of sixty Norman knights when he made his first bid for the throne of Gwynedd in 1075. Following his ejection the same year, his deposer Trahaearn ap Caradog was unable to hold back the Normans of Chester who raided into the Llyn peninsula. The Chester forces were aided by men from Powys under Gwrgan ap Seisyll.

In 1098 Robert de Belleme became earl of Shrewsbury. To maintain his security he sought agreements with his Welsh neighbours. Powys was granted to Cadwgan ap Bleddyn, and he and his brothers Maredudd and Iorwerth became Robert's vassals. A further agreement of non-aggression was made with Gruffudd ap Cynan in Gwynedd at the same time. During the succession dispute of 1100, Earl Robert supported Robert Curthose against Henry I and therefore incurred the new king's wrath. In 1103 he was summoned to face charges but instead he prepared for war, fortifying his lands and calling on his Welsh allies. Henry I needed not only to reduce Robert's castles, but to wean the Welsh away from him. He offered Iorwerth dominion over all of south and central Wales still in native hands, an offer which was gladly accepted. When Iorwerth's troops began to fight against him, Robert's power was broken and he surrendered.

In the south of Wales little further Norman expansion had occurred since the death of William fitz Osbern. This may have been partially due to an unwillingness on William I's part to sanction any border raiding, in case any of his lords became too powerful as Earl Roger had. During this time the dominant lord of south Wales, Rhys ap Tewdwr of Deheubarth, allied himself to the exiled Gruffudd of Gwynedd. In 1081 with a large Viking army they were victorious at the battle of Mynydd Carn. Soon after William I led an army to St. Davids in Dyfed, and there met Rhys ap Tewdwr. This advance may well have been a show of strength, to point out to Rhys that William was watching Wales carefully and would act if he deemed it necessary. He would not tolerate the Welsh using Vikings against his Normans, should they think to do so. Domesday Book records that soon after this, Rhys paid forty pounds to William I for his tenure of Deheubarth, and became his vassal.[9] This would free him of Norman intervention at least until William I's death.

William I therefore achieved peace along the border by establishing a balance of power. By making Rhys his vassal he negated the threat from Deheubarth, and by refusing to appoint another earl of Hereford he ensured that there was no one on his side of the border who was strong enough to oppose the status-quo. The death of William I in 1087 ended this agreement, and the Normans once more began to make incursions into south Wales. In 1093, as Brut y Tywysogyon states: 'Rhys ap Tewdwr, king of the South, was slain by Frenchmen who were inhabiting Brycheiniog - with whom fell the kingdom of the Britons.'[10] The death of Rhys left south Wales open to a new wave of invasion, spearheaded by Bernard de Neufmarche, who heavily fortified Brycheiniog, building Brecon castle. Now that Rhys was gone, south Wales seemed ripe for the taking.

In the north of Wales there had been no accord between William I and the native rulers, and Norman incursions continued apace. Earl Hugh's foremost lieutenant was his cousin Robert of Rhuddlan, another of Edward the Confessor's favourites, returned after the conquest to make his name. From 1073 onwards he began to push along the coast of north Wales, defeating first Bleddyn ap Cynfyn and then Trahaearn ap Caradog, so that by 1080 he had reached Deganwy, which he fortified. He probably had an agreement with Bleddyn ap Cynfyn whilst he lived, and therefore made no advances upon Gwynedd at this time. The defeat of Trahaearn in 1081 aided the Norman expansion, and by 1086, with Gruffudd secure in prison, Earl Hugh had captured all northern Flintshire with Robert as his chief tenant. West of the Clwyd Robert held the cantrefs of Rhos and Rhufoniog as his own, and paid forty pounds to William I for the tenancy of north Wales, or Gwynedd and Arwystli. What he was effectively doing was claiming the kingship of Gwynedd. Arwystli was at this time in dispute, for though it had been granted to Robert, it was held by Earl Roger of Shrewsbury.

Thus by William I's death much of north Wales was held by Robert and Hugh. The Cheshire plain was shielded by this frontier. Ordericus Vitalis' description of Robert of Rhuddlan could well have stood as a blue print for many of the Marcher lords of the day,

> The warlike marcher lord often fought against this unruly people and slew many in battle after battle. After driving back the native Britons in fierce combat he enlarged his territories and built a strongly fortified castle on the hill of Deganwy which is near to the sea. For fifteen years he harried the Welsh mercilessly, invaded the lands of men who when they still enjoyed their original liberty had owed nothing to the Normans, pursued them through woods and marshes and over steep mountains and found different ways of securing their submission.[11]

His illustrious career was cut short in either 1088 or 1093 when he was killed in a raid on Deganwy. However this did not halt the Norman advance. North Wales was granted to Earl Hugh who promptly advanced along the coast. Castles were constructed on Anglesey and at Caernarfon and Bangor. In 1092 a Breton, Herve, was made bishop in Gwynedd and the monastery of Chester was granted lands on Anglesey and in Rhos.

By this time the advance in south Wales had resumed, and as Bernard de Neufmarche consolidated his hold in Brycheiniog Earl Roger swept from Shrewsbury into Ceredigion and built Cardigan castle. Dyfed was also raided, and the castles of Carmarthen and Pembroke were constructed. At the same time, Robert fitz Hamo commenced the conquest of Glamorgan, establishing Cardiff and Newport as principal bases. No attempt was as yet being made to subjugate the highlands of the south, and fitz Hamo's attacks were all centred on the coastal lowlands. In these campaigns the Normans were attempting to tailor their tactics to Welsh conditions. All of Earl Hugh's castles were garrisoned with archers and companies of light horse, and all along the border companies of light horse were raised. They were intended to pursue and destroy Welsh forces, acting as mounted infantry if necessary, tasks the heavy cavalry could not perform in Welsh terrain.[12]

However, the Norman tactics were found wanting, and the sudden burst of forward movement came to an abrupt halt in 1094. Alarmed at the great sweeps from Shrewsbury and Chester the Welsh rebelled while the Normans were over extended and had not properly consolidated their gains. Hugh of Chester and his bishop were driven out of north Wales and Anglesey, while in the south, Ceredigion and Dyfed were freed except for the castle of Pembroke, which could be supplied by sea and held on under its castellan, Gerald of Windsor. The whole of the border land was ravaged by Welsh raids and Norman counter attacks were ambushed and defeated, as at Aber Llech in Brycheiniog in 1095. A royal campaign of that year achieved nothing as the Welsh melted away before the advancing host, and the action continued on into 1096. A second royal campaign of 1097 also failed to achieve any significant gains, but by now the rebellion, conducted in a piecemeal fashion, began to die and the Normans regained the initiative.

This was due in no small part to the number of castles that had been constructed. They had been an important part of the Norman strategy from the beginning, enabling them to hold down territory without recourse to massive armies, with little need to bring the Welsh to battle. Though much territory had been lost, the majority of the castles held out, and as the Normans regained the initiative, they were used as bases for reoccupation. By the death of William II in 1100 much of Dyfed, Ceredigion and Ystrad Tywi had been recovered. It was in the north that the rebellion had its greatest effects. In 1098 a joint campaign from Chester and Shrewsbury was launched to recover Gwynedd and Anglesey. The Normans marched to the Menai straits and there bought off Gruffudd ap Cynan's Viking mercenaries. Anglesey was heavily ravaged but Hugh of Shrewsbury was killed. The Normans withdrew, knowing their position west of the Conwy would always be too exposed, and did not occupy this area again until the conquest of 1282.

By 1100 the initial explosion of conquest had died down. Large tracts of

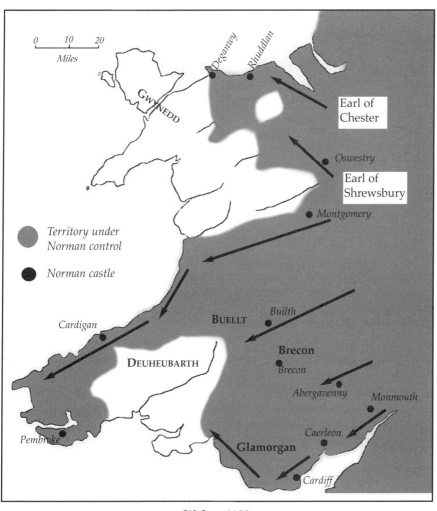

Wales: 1100

lowland Wales were in the hands of the invaders and the Marches had been established. These lordships took on a unique character, being 'Essentially Welsh principalities in Norman hands.'[13] The liberties of the Lords Marcher derived both from the power and prerogatives of a Welsh prince, and from those of a feudal lord. They were still vassals of the king, however, and he could intervene if they could be seen to threaten the crown in any way.

The surrender of Robert of Belleme in 1103 had altered the entire complexion of the Marches. By then Earl Hugh of Chester had died leaving a seven-year-old boy as his heir, and Hereford was still in abeyance. The days of the independent earls were over, considered too much of a threat. In 1103, just as in the 1050s, an alliance of an independent magnate and a powerful Welsh lord had threatened the security of central government. This could not be allowed to happen again, and Henry I determined that marcher affairs were ultimately to be governed by himself.

Notes

1. M. Prestwich, *Armies and warfare in the middle ages. The English experience*, New Haven, Yale University Press, 1996, p.18.
2. R. A. Brown, 'The Battle of Hastings', in M. Strickland, (ed.) *Anglo-Norman Warfare*, Woodbridge, Boydell Press, 1993, pp.172–174.
3. R. A. Brown, 'The Battle of Hastings', in M. Strickland, (ed.) *Anglo-Norman Warfare*, Woodbridge, Boydell Press, 1993, p.171.
4. C. W. Hollister, *Monarchy, magnates and institutions in the Anglo-Norman world*, London, Hambledon Press, 1986, p.7.
5. *English Historical Documents*, pp.170-1.
6. C. W. Hollister, *Monarchy, magnates and institutions in the Anglo-Norman world*, London, Hambledon Press, 1986, pp.11-12.
7. C. W. Hollister, *Monarchy, magnates and institutions in the Anglo-Norman world*, London, Hambledon Press, 1986, p.12.
8. J. O. Prestwich, 'The military households of the Norman kings', in M. Strickland (ed.) *Anglo-Norman warfare*, Woodbridge, Boydell Press, 1993, p.107.
9. J. E. Lloyd, 'Wales and the coming of the Normans', *Transactions of the Honourable Society of Cymmrodorion*, 1899-1900, p.151.
10. *Brut y Tywysogion*, p.19.
11. M. Chibnall, (ed.) *Ordericus Vitalis. The ecclesiastical history* v.IV, Oxford, Oxford University Press, 1973, p.139.
12. F. C. Suppe, *Military institutions on the Welsh marches*, Woodbridge, Boydell Press, 1994, p.18.
13. J. Le Patourel, *The Norman empire*, Oxford, Oxford University Press, 1978, p.64.

Chapter 4
The Twelfth and Thirteenth Centuries

The twelfth and thirteenth centuries were a period of royal campaigns and Welsh offensives. The Anglo-Norman lords found themselves on the defensive in the face of strengthening opposition, but the Welsh could not eject the invaders from their lands. Throughout the period the position of the crown played a major role, and by and large it was the power and will of the crown which drove affairs with the Welsh. The Marcher lords were often harnessed to the crown and used as implements of the royal policy.

From the beginning of his reign Henry I sought control over Wales rather than conquest. He was satisfied with stability rather than dominion and preferred to exercise overlordship rather than attempt direct lordship. To these ends he established royal lordships in the south to serve as centres of his authority and power. William fitz Baldwin had constructed the castle of Rhyd-y-Gors on the Tywi in 1095. It had been destroyed in the Welsh offensives of that year, but by 1109 the castle and the territory around it was in royal ownership, and it became the lordship of Carmarthen. It was the chief base of royal power in the south of Wales, a place from where the authority and justice of the crown would radiate outwards across the territory of marcher and native lord alike. This important lordship was entrusted by Henry to Earl Walter of Gloucester.[1]

With this lordship seeing to the security and stability of the south, Henry turned his attention to the north. Norman authority had suffered most here during the fighting of the close of the eleventh century, to the extent that Norman power west of the Clwyd was wiped out. Henry had no lordships on which to base his power, and so he turned to the native princes as instruments of his might. Initially he attempted to cultivate the lords of Powys, and make it a client kingdom under crown authority. However, dynastic disputes tore Powys apart and it soon became clear that it was not strong enough to serve Henry's purpose.

Throughout this time the lord of Gwynedd, Gruffudd ap Cynan had been quietly re building both his power and his lordship after his long struggle to acquire them.[2] So successful was he by 1114, Henry decided that it was time for a campaign against him. He led an army against Gwynedd, passing through Powys as he went, to demonstrate his power to its lords, Owain ap

Cadwgan and Maredudd ap Bleddyn. Both sought terms with him. The demonstration was sufficient for Gruffudd, who submitted and paid fines to Henry as his overlord.[3] By receiving the submission of Gruffudd Henry was able to stabilise the situation in the north as he had in the south, though he still faced sporadic troubles during the rest of his reign. In 1116 Gruffudd ap Rhys of Deheubarth rebelled against Norman overlordship, but his brief uprising came to little, chiefly due to his inability to capture castles.[4] A campaign was also needed against Maredudd ap Bleddyn in 1121. It was successful and Maredudd was cowed into submission once more. For much of his reign Henry's overlordship was unchallenged. Such was his authority over both natives and marchers that Brut y Tywysogyon described him as 'The man against whom no one could be of avail save God himself'.[5]

As Henry's reign waned, the period of relative peace gradually came to a close. In 1134 a damaging raid was launched into Shropshire and Caus castle was destroyed.[6] Henry died in 1135 and his overlordship, personal in nature, died with him. Anglo Norman and native lords who had been held in check by the forceful king found themselves free to act, and violence flared across all of Wales. Norman troops were defeated by Hywel ap Maredudd near Swansea in 1136, and in April of the same year Richard Fitz Gilbert de Clare was murdered.[7] This was followed by a swift invasion of Ceredigion by Owain and Cadwaladr of Gwynedd, who in a series of campaigns during 1136 ejected the Normans from the whole of the lordship save for Cardigan castle itself. A relief army numbering some 3000 men was smashed at Crug Mawr near Cardigan in October. In this battle, according to the Brut, the Welsh army included 'Two thousand mailed horsemen ready for battle'.[8] It is clear that the Welsh lords were learning from their Norman foes, and adapting their tactics when the situation favoured them. The following year the army of Gwynedd seized Carmarthen.

The Anglo-Norman response to these catastrophes was non existent, for in 1138 open war broke out between King Stephen and the Angevin faction which contained many of the Marcher lords, Earl Robert of Gloucester foremost amongst them. This meant that Stephen could not fight back against the Welsh, and any counter attack had to be made by individual lords. In 1144 Hugh Mortimer succeeded in re- taking Maelienydd and in the following year Gilbert Fitz Gilbert de Clare rebuilt Carmarthen.[9] By 1150 Owain Gwynedd had advanced to the border with Cheshire after defeating Powysian opposition as well as English. Between 1150 and 1153 Maredudd and Rhys ap Gruffudd of Deheubarth captured Ceredigion from the men of Gwynedd. This in-fighting between the Welsh lords at this time should not be seen as a sign of weakness, however, but merely the restoration of the status-quo between native realms. Gwynedd's position in Ceredigion was unnatural, and Deheubarth was restoring the usual stability by ejecting them. However, this warfare within Wales had the effect at this time of blunting the Welsh offensives against the Normans.

The task of stabilising England kept Henry II busy from his accession in 1154 until three years later, but then he turned his attention to Wales. In 1157 he led a large royal army from Chester, determined to force Owain Gwynedd back from the Cheshire border. The Earl of Chester was at this time a minor, and this is the likely reason why Henry chose to lead a campaign. Owain needed to be notified that Chester was not a viable target for his attentions. He took up positions at Basingwerk to face the royal host, whilst the king led a smaller force in an effort to turn the Welsh flank. This action almost ended in disaster as the force was ambushed and Henry himself was in grave danger. But his flanking manoeuvre was successful and Owain withdrew. In the meanwhile a royal fleet was defeated as it landed on Anglesey against orders, but at this point Henry and Owain came to terms. Owain did homage and withdrew west of the Clwyd once more.[10]

With the north again secure, attention was turned to the south, where Rhys ap Gruffudd had gained control of Deheubarth. He initially capitulated to the crown in 1157 but was busy the following two years, besieging Carmarthen castle in 1159. In 1162 he captured Llandovery, and Henry II launched a campaign, his fourth since 1158, against him. Rhys was captured at Pencader and taken to England. At Woodstock he and Owain Gwynedd did homage to Henry and Rhys was restored to his lands. In 1164 he ravaged Ceredigion again and as Henry prepared a massive campaign of retribution Rhys and Owain banded together against the threat, as did Owain Cyfeiliog and Iorwerth Goch of Powys, and Cadwallon ap Madog and Einion Clud from south Wales.

Owain assumed overall command of this Welsh alliance, and in response Henry expanded his plans. He advanced from Shrewsbury in August 1165 but the weather worsened and the expedition became bogged down in the Berwyn mountains. Short of food and unable to resupply his large force due to the rain Henry had to withdraw. This was the last campaign Henry tried, having come to the conclusion that direct force could not solve the problem. For the rest of the decade Henry faced insurrection, Cardigan castle finally fell to Rhys in 1166 as he consolidated his authority in Ceredigion, Ystrad-Tywi and much of Dyfed. The same year Owain destroyed Basingwerk castle and in 1167 he besieged and took Rhuddlan, extending his power to the Dee once more. He died in 1170, and the situation eased in the north, as his sons fought amongst themselves.

The death of Owain left Rhys as the sole great lord in native Wales. His position was strengthened in that the Norman invasion of Ireland drew off many of his enemies and their retinues, including Earl Richard of Pembroke.[11] At this juncture, in 1170, Henry and Rhys finally came to terms. Rhys did homage to Henry and acted as justiciar in south Wales for the rest of Henry's reign. Troops were sent by the Lord Rhys, as he came to be known, in 1173 to aid the king in his Normandy campaign, and again in 1174 against both Earl William of Derby and Louis VII of France. By the fragmentation of Gwynedd and coming to terms with Rhys, Henry II had finally achieved the stability he desired. Much territory formerly held by the Normans was still in Welsh hands, but this was an acceptable price to pay for understanding and detente.

Not all was peaceful during this time and sporadic violence, such as the sacking of Cardiff and Kenfig in 1185, arose to threaten the accord. However such was the relationship that Henry and Rhys had forged, they were able to resolve any disputes and remain cordial. Under the government of Richard I this detente broke down. Once again the relationship had been personal between Rhys and Henry, and the governors appointed by Richard seemed indifferent to the benefits of renewing it. Rhys led several raids on Anglo-Norman lordships, and in response the Marcher lords resumed their aggression. In 1196 the Justiciar Hubert Walter laid siege to Welshpool in Powys, and a Welsh army was destroyed at Painscastle by Geoffrey Fitz Peter in 1198. The crown was once again assuming an aggressive policy towards Wales. Meanwhile after Rhys' death in 1197, the balance of power in Wales again shifted to the north.

King John assumed the throne in 1199. By now Gwynedd was held by Llywelyn ab Iorwerth, a rival of Gwenwynwyn ab Owain Cyfeiliog of southern Powys. Initially John gave his support to Llywelyn, but then withdrew it in 1200 only to restore it in 1201 and make a treaty with Gwynedd. In it Llywelyn and the magnates of native Wales all swore fealty to John as their overlord. Three years later Llywelyn married John's illegitimate daughter Joan, but these cordial relations broke down in 1210 due to Llywelyn's dealings with the disgraced Marcher William de Braose. John determined upon a campaign to bring Gwynedd back to heel. The initial campaign of May 1211 from Chester turned back due to lack of supplies, but a second in July marched rapidly from Oswestry to Bangor which was ravaged.[12] John had the support of numerous Welsh lords who were alarmed at Llywelyn's ambition. The ruler of Gwynedd sought terms, and lost much. All of Llywelyn's lands between the Conwy and Dee were surrendered. A heavy fine of cattle and horses was exacted, and it was

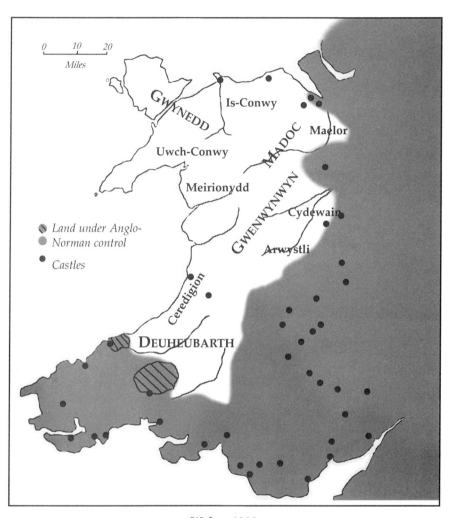

Wales: 1200

agreed that if Llywelyn had no heir by Joan, Gwynedd would escheat to the crown upon his death.

John's campaign left him in a position of power unmatched by an English king in Wales. Yet this position proved to be his downfall as he began to install royal officials across Wales. The native lords, alarmed at this unforseen eventuality, threw their weight behind Gwynedd to eject the Normans from their acquisitions. In response John planned a campaign on a massive scale. The feudal host was called upon, and troops were raised in Scotland, Ireland and Flanders. Also some 8000 engineers were levied in support, and it seemed that John intended nothing short of conquest. The campaign was never launched, as Joan warned the king of a plot by disgruntled barons to have him kidnapped or captured by the Welsh.[13]

In 1212 Llywelyn allied with King Philip Augustus of France against John, signing a treaty of mutual support.[14] In 1215, taking full advantage of the civil war in England, Llywelyn gathered an army which included contingents from every great lord of Wales, most of whom served in person. Sweeping around south Wales, in December the castles of Carmarthen, Kidwelly, Llanstephan, St. Clears, Laugharne, Narberth, Newport, Cardigan and Cilgerran all fell. The only crown footholds remaining in the south were Haverfordwest and Pembroke. Early in 1216 Llywelyn presided over a partition of these conquered lordships amongst his allies.[15] By the death of John later the same year he was undisputed master of native Wales.

The government of Henry III came to terms with Llywelyn in 1218, and he did homage to Henry as his overlord. It had been his intention that he should do homage on behalf of all the Welsh lords, but this was unacceptable to England, who saw Llywelyn as leader of the Welsh but not their lord. It became the overriding aim of the princes of Gwynedd from now on to have their authority as overlord of Wales recognised by the crown.

Relations between Henry and Llywelyn were generally good, though the directly opposing aims of the two were bound to cause friction at times. Three royal campaigns, under the guidance of the Justiciar Hubert de Burgh were launched, in 1223, 1228 and 1231, but only the first one achieved anything of note, recapturing Cardigan and Carmarthen. In a quiet way the crown recovered from the defeats of John's reign, Montgomery was taken into royal hands in 1223 and with Cardigan and Carmarthen, would serve as a base for future action. Chester was annexed to the crown in 1237, its last earl having died without issue. Despite Llywelyn's best efforts, and the numerous campaigns he instigated as a spur to royal tardiness, Henry never granted the lord of Gwynedd the recognition he sought, and forbade anyone

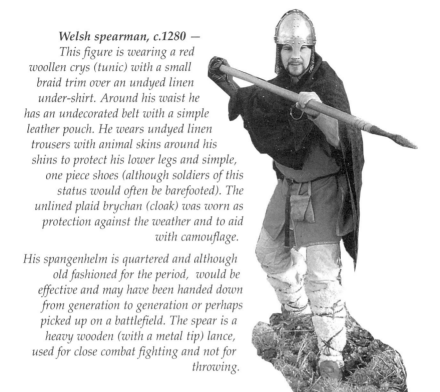

Welsh spearman, c.1280 —
This figure is wearing a red
woollen crys (tunic) with a small
braid trim over an undyed linen
under-shirt. Around his waist he
has an undecorated belt with a simple
leather pouch. He wears undyed linen
trousers with animal skins around his
shins to protect his lower legs and simple,
one piece shoes (although soldiers of this
status would often be barefooted). The
unlined plaid brychan (cloak) was worn as
protection against the weather and to aid
with camouflage.

His spangenhelm is quartered and although
old fashioned for the period, would be
effective and may have been handed down
from generation to generation or perhaps
picked up on a battlefield. The spear is a
heavy wooden (with a metal tip) lance,
used for close combat fighting and not for
throwing.

to give their homage and fealty to any but the crown. When in 1238 the lords of Wales were summoned to Strata Florida to swear homage to Dafydd, Llywelyn's heir, all they gave him was their allegiance. Llywelyn ab Iorwerth died in 1240 with his chief aim unachieved.

Dafydd ap Llywelyn became prince of Gwynedd in April 1240 and the crown quickly sprang from its period of relative inactivity. He and all the native lords were summoned to do homage to the king, and in the Treaty of Gloucester most of Llywelyn's territorial gains were stripped away. The Marcher lords instantly went on to the offensive, especially in upland Glamorgan and Brecon, where the Clares and Bohuns extended their authority. A royal campaign reinforced the pressure on Dafydd in 1241, and caused his surrender at Gwern Eigron. This, followed closely by the Treaty

Welsh footsoldier, c.1280 —
Clothed in a manner very like that of the
spearman from the same period, he is
wearing simple shoes, similar to Viking 'turn
shoes'. The trousers are of heavy linen as is his
crys (tunic). An undecorated belt hold a simple
skin pouch and a small drinking horn. The
brychan (cloak) is unlined and although of a
different colour to that worn by the spearman, serves
the same purpose.

The mailed glove is crude enough to be home-made
although it could be a captured piece, perhaps looted
off a battlefield. The sword is of an old design with a
'brazil nut' pommel, but the cross-guard is up to
date for the late 13th century. Again this is
probably a captured piece.

The hair is cropped short to keep it out of the eyes
when fighting (no helm to keep it out of the way)
and to prevent it tangling in trees and bushes
when in woodland.

of London later that year saw Dafydd lose all of his father's gains. Deganwy castle was surrendered to the crown, and Gruffudd, Dafydd's half brother was handed over, and his rights to a portion of Gwynedd acknowledged. He was lodged in the Tower of London, a hostage for Dafydd's good faith. If he misbehaved or died without issue then Gwynedd would escheat to the crown.

The death of Gruffudd, while trying to escape from captivity in 1244, changed the situation markedly. With the crown hostage gone Dafydd rebelled, threatening to retake all he had lost. A campaign against him from Chester in 1245 failed due to logistical inadequacies but a second was opened by Nicholas de Molis in the summer of 1246 from Carmarthen. During this time Dafydd died and the other lords sullenly returned to the crown, leaving the new lords of Gwynedd, Owain and Llywelyn ap Gruffudd, to fight on alone. A royal campaign penetrated into Gwynedd and the brothers sought terms. In the Treaty of Woodstock of 30 April 1247 Owain and Llywelyn were stripped of everything save for Gwynedd west of the Conwy, which was now to be held by military service and in chief of the crown. Intransigence would result in forfeiture to the crown. Henry further strengthened the position of the crown in north Wales at this time by taking the four cantrefs of Gwynedd east of the Conwy into royal lordship.

The power of Gwynedd was smashed and could not be repaired in the foreseeable future, as a further two sons of Gruffudd, Dafydd and Rhodri, were as yet too young to claim portions of their uncle's patrimony, but waited to do so. It seemed that from its position of total authority, the crown would support their claims.

It was not to be so. Llywelyn ap Gruffudd, second of the brothers, was not satisfied with his portion of his uncle's patrimony following the treaty of 1247. He was an able and shrewd man, and began to make efforts to extend his power. In 1250 he mad a formal 'Confederacy and union,' with the native lord of Bromfield, Gruffudd ap Madog, 'Against all men great and small'. In 1251 Llywelyn and Owain made a treaty with Maredudd ap Rhys Gryg of Dryslwyn and Rhys Fychan of Ystrad-Tywi. As all these men were vassals of the crown, the pacts should have included clauses reserving their fealty to the king. No such clauses were inserted.[16] A network of alliances was being set up for a future challenge to the overlordship of the crown.

In 1254, the county of Chester and the royal lands in Wales; the Perfeddwlad, the lordships of Montgomery, Builth, Cardigan, and Carmarthen, were given to Henry III's son the Lord Edward. His officials were emplaced across these areas and began to rule, in his name, in a most unwise manner. They were indifferent to local customs and traditions, Welsh sensibilities were ignored and the Welsh themselves alienated.

The worsening situation between Owain, who supported Dafydd's claim to a share of Gwynedd; and Llywelyn, who did not, was resolved in 1255 when at the battle of Bryn Derwin the army of Owain and Dafydd was smashed and Llywelyn established himself as the sole ruler of Gwynedd. Both Owain and Dafydd were imprisoned, Dafydd to be released and to join with Llywelyn a year later, and Owain to languish there until 1277. Rhodri had his claim nullified with promises to buy him out, though this was not in fact done until 1278.

The events in native Wales and the royal lordships came together a year after Bryn Derwin, when in November 1256 the people of the Perfeddwlad, seething with discontent at the mis-rule of Edward's officials, called for aid. Within a week Llywelyn and his ally Maredudd had raised the entire area. Only the royal castles of Diserth and Deganwy held out. By the end of the year Meirionnydd, Ceredigion and Gwerthrynion were all in Llywelyn's hands, and further offensives in the following two years saw southern Powys overrun and the lords of northern Powys defect to the prince of Gwynedd. Royal counter offensives were ineffectual, and Stephen Bauzan was defeated at Cymerau in 1257. In 1258 a gathering of the native lords was held where Llywelyn was titled prince of Wales, and the lords of Wales did him homage. 'His assumption of the title was more than a gesture. it was both the answer to a challenge and a declaration of purpose.'[17] That challenge had been issued when Edward received into his hands the royal lordships. At a stroke this made him the single greatest land holder in all of Wales: a direct challenge to the power of Gwynedd. Events of 1255–58 had effectively answered that challenge.

Foremost on Llywelyn's mind following his successes was to have recognition from the crown. To these ends he sought peace with Henry III, offering him £16,500 in 1259 for peace. Henry, unable to counter attack due to domestic troubles, nevertheless was determined not to yield to Welsh pressure and only granted a truce. It was broken in 1260 when, as a spur to negotiations Llywelyn seized the lordship of Builth from Roger Mortimer, and destroyed the castle. Two years later a local rising against Mortimer in the lordship of Maelienydd destroyed Cefnllys castle. Llywelyn joined in and rapidly conquered the whole lordship, and followed this with further campaigns in Blaenllynfi and Brecon in response to local risings. In August and September 1263 the beleaguered castles of Diserth and Deganwy finally fell. Following these successes Gruffudd ap Gwenwynwyn of southern Powys, the only Welsh lord who was not a confederate of the prince of Gwynedd finally came to terms with him and did homage. This was partly to avoid the wrath of the ascendant prince of Gwynedd, and partly because Gruffudd was himself having trouble with his marcher neighbours at the time. During the unrest and civil war in England which blunted any hope of a counter attack, Llywelyn gave his support to the baronial faction. Welsh troops were present at sieges of Marcher fortresses in 1264. In 1265 Earl Simon de Montfort, recognising Llywelyn's support, granted him the Treaty of Pipton. Llywelyn was recognised as prince and in return he would pay Simon's government £20,000. However the tide had turned against Simon, who was in no position to grant treaties. Llywelyn must have known this, and only used Pipton as a marker, an indication to the royalists of what they needed to grant him in return for his cooperation.

Henry was in no position or mood to resume hostilities with Wales following Simon's death in 1265, and the attempts of the Marchers to regain lost territory were easily beaten off. Thus in 1267, following negotiations headed by the papal legate cardinal Ottobuono, the Treaty of Montgomery was signed between Henry III and Llywelyn ap Gruffudd. Llywelyn was confirmed as the hereditary prince of Wales, and granted the homage of all the native lords apart from his one-time ally Maredudd ap Rhys Gryg. He had withdrawn from his alliance in 1259. It was clear that he feared Llywelyn's overlordship and did not wish to be a part of it. However, it was agreed that his fealty could be bought at a later date for the sum of 5000 marks. The lordships of Brecon, Gwerthrynion, Builth, Ceri and Cedewain, along with the Perfeddwlad were all ceded to Gwynedd. Llywelyn held Elfael and Moldsdale though they were not included in the treaty, and Maelienydd was recognised as being in dispute with Roger Mortimer, who was allowed to repair Cefnllys whilst the matter was looked into. In return for all this Llywelyn was to do homage to Henry III, and pay the sum of 25,000 marks in instalments of 3,000 per annum, after an initial payment of 5,000.

In only twelve years the position of the crown in Wales had been obliterated. Llywelyn used the unrest in England to extend his own power so that a weakened crown could not challenge it, and, using this strategy, he was ultimately successful where no other Welsh lord had been before. Llywelyn was still a vassal of the king, but he created a principality in which, with the exception of Maredudd ap Rhys Gryg, he was the only tenant in chief. The lords of Wales now looked to him as their overlord. This new principality was by no means the entirety of Wales, for the marcher lords still held considerable territories, and the royal honours of Cardigan and Carmarthen loomed on Llywelyn's flank.

Trouble began with the marchers immediately. They had lost a great deal and were determined to recoup their losses. In January 1267 Earl Gilbert of Gloucester imprisoned Gruffudd ap Rhys of Senghennydd, assuming the commote for himself and strengthening his hold upon it by commencing construction of Caerphilly castle. This was seen by the new prince of Wales as direct provocation. Though in Glamorgan and thus outside the principality, Gruffudd was a native lord and Llywelyn argued that he should hold his homage, not the earl of Gloucester. The Treaty of Montgomery did yield to Llywelyn the homage of 'All the Welsh barons of Wales,' but it did not stipulate who these barons were, or for that matter what Wales was. Clearly the Senghennydd matter was a controversial issue

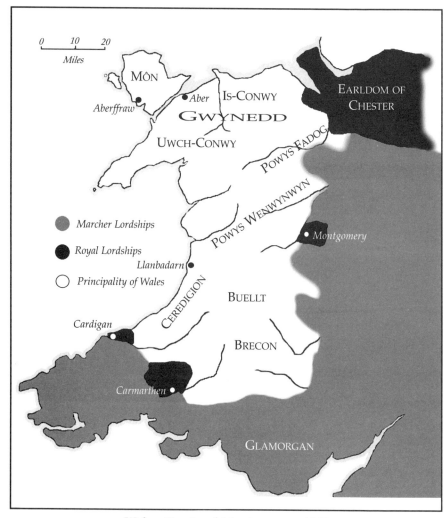

Wales: Treaty of Montgomery, 1267

and negotiations were undertaken. By 1270 little headway had been made and Llywelyn destroyed Caerphilly. It was rebuilt and Llywelyn became embroiled in a war with Gilbert over upland Gwent and Glamorgan. By 1272 Gilbert had gained the upper hand and at this time, the dispossessed lord of Brecon, Humphrey de Bohun joined in. He wished to regain his lordship and made numerous incursions supported by Roger Mortimer, who was one of the regents ruling England in King Edward's absence. Thus the actions of the Marchers had governmental approval, and to worsen matters further for the prince of Wales Mortimer made incursions into the middle March on his own accord, intent on regaining Maelienydd. Many of the Welsh of Elfael and Maelienydd were only held to Llywelyn's overlordship through threats and fines, their loyalty was dubious. Against the forces of the marchers and the internal dissent within the disputed lordships, Llywelyn was hard pressed to retain them.

Throughout this time relations with the crown fell apart. After the treaty of 1267 Henry III had washed his hands of Welsh affairs and was content to let his ministers, led by the Lord Edward, deal with matters. Edward was the only man with authority enough to deal with both sides in the disputes, and did appear to be sympathetic towards the prince. His departure on crusade in 1270 meant that matters worsened. Henry III died two years later and the council headed by Mortimer took over. The payments due for the treaty ceased, a sign of the trouble which lay ahead.

In 1274 Dafydd ap Gruffudd and Gruffudd ap Gwenwynwyn plotted to murder the prince, and when foiled they fled to England where they obtained asylum. Llywelyn refused to do homage to Edward's representatives in 1273, and did not attend the coronation in 1274. He was summoned to Shrewsbury in November 1274 to do homage, but Edward was ill and the meeting was cancelled. Following this Dafydd and Gruffudd arrived in England, and the following year Llywelyn's bride Eleanor de Montfort was detained by Edward. Llywelyn refused to do homage until his grievances were addressed, Eleanor released and the fugitives handed over. Four summonses to do homage at Chester, Westminster and Winchester, were ignored, and Edward's attitude hardened also. He may well have wished to redress Llywelyn's grievances, holding Eleanor, Dafydd and Gruffudd as bargaining pieces, but now confrontation was inevitable. As overlord, Edward was bound to deal with any complaints his vassal may have, but as Llywelyn had done no homage Edward was not bound to answer any complaint. Neither Edward nor Llywelyn could back down from the stance they had taken, and on November 12th 1276 Llywelyn was condemned as a recalcitrant vassal and war was declared.

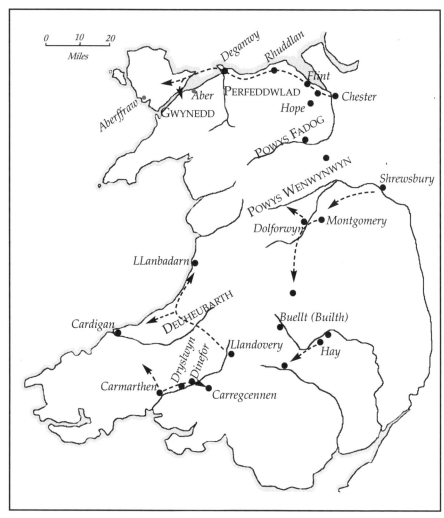

Wales: First War of Independence, 1276–77

Three military commands were created at Chester, Shrewsbury and Carmarthen, where armies were raised and prepared to attack the principality from three sides and pin Llywelyn into Snowdonia. Troops from Chester cowed the lords of northern Powys into submission, and the castle of Dinas Bran was burned to keep it from English hands. Llywelyn's new castle of Dolforwyn fell in April 1277 after a siege of eight days, and by May Builth was again in English hands. The forces from Carmarthen, aided by Rhys ap Maredudd of Dryslwyn, retook the castles of the Tywi valley as the lords of Deheubarth surrendered. By July the armies had retaken all but Gwynedd itself. The main army from Chester pushed along the coast, reaching the river Conwy by 29 August, establishing the castles of Flint and Rhuddlan as it went. The capture of Anglesey by naval assault at a stroke outflanked the Welsh positions in Snowdonia and robbed them of much needed food supplies. With winter drawing on, Llywelyn felt compelled to seek terms.

The Treaty of Aberconwy was made at the end of the year, and the power so recently ceded to Llywelyn ap Gruffudd was stripped away. He lost all of Wales apart from Gwynedd west of the Conwy and the homage of five lords, though the title of prince was still his. Anglesey was held for a rent of 1,000 marks per annum, and would escheat to the crown in the event of Llywelyn failing to produce an heir. A fine of £50,000 was to be handed over as recompense for his mis-behaviour, and ten hostages would ensure he did not transgress again. Owain was released from prison and settled on lands in Llyn, and Dafydd too was reconciled, though Edward provided lands for him from his conquests. He was given the two cantrefs of Rhufoniog and Dyffryn Clwyd and the lordship of Hope. Llywelyn did homage at Rhuddlan and again at Christmas in London, and the fine and the rent for Anglesey were remitted, replaced by a payment of 500 marks per annum until the arrears from the Treaty of Montgomery were paid off. Edward I's victory in 1277 had been complete and sweeping: 'It involved much more than bringing a recalcitrant vassal to heel; it represented a major redistribution of power in favour of the English, and in particular of the king, throughout Wales'.[18] Territory which was captured was restored to its Marcher owners or retained by the crown, Builth was taken up as a royal lordship. Castles were built or restored at Flint, Builth, Rhuddlan and Aberystwyth, along with Ruthin, Hope and Hawarden to consolidate the resumption of royal authority.

The war was a disaster, and the Treaty of Conwy which ended it a humiliation. But there was little reason why Llywelyn should accept it as a final verdict: in Anglo-Welsh warfare final verdicts came only with death.[19]

Llywelyn was still prince of Wales and though small, his principality was in many respects more secure than that created in 1267. His borders were clearly defined, he did not have to rely on other lords with wavering loyalty, and neither did he have to shoulder the crippling financial burdens the greater principality had entailed. Both king and prince seemed keen to avoid further hostilities; Edward even stood as Llywelyn's best man at his wedding to Eleanor de Montfort. The accord did not last long.

As in the 1250s royal officials who had been emplaced in the retaken lordships, most notably in the cantrefs of Perfeddwlad not given to Dafydd, ruled with a heavy hand. Welshmen who had deserted Llywelyn in 1276–77 began to realise that his overlordship was more palatable than that of the crown after all, and before long the prince of Wales was again creating a network of alliances.

It was not Llywelyn ap Gruffudd who began the war of 1282, however, but his brother Dafydd. At one point Edward had contemplated deposing Llywelyn and setting Dafydd in his place, but the rapid surrender at the end of 1277 had changed his mind. Dafydd was therefore denied the prize he sought. Two cantrefs and the lordship of Hope was not reward enough, especially as royal officials interfered in his affairs. This situation was repeated across Wales, and other lords than Dafydd soon came to resent such interference. Furthermore, Eleanor de Montfort was now pregnant and Dafydd must have seen his last hopes of ever becoming prince slipping away. It was in the Perfeddwlad once more that the rebellion began. Hawarden castle was stormed on 21 March 1282. Oswestry was raided one day later, and soon after the castles of Aberystwyth, Llandovery and Carreg Cennan were taken.

Edward was unprepared for a national rising and had to hastily plan to counter it. Soon after hearing of the rebellion he decided upon a strategy similar to that of the last war, but on a larger scale, 'His campaign of 1277 had been little more than a brief military promenade, followed by successful negotiations. The second Welsh war, was to be a very different matter.'[20] Nothing short of the out-right conquest of the principality would suffice. Preparations began in March with the establishment of the three commands based upon Chester, Montgomery and Carmarthen once more. In April a summons to 158 vassals to serve 'At our wages' was issued, and feudal summonses followed. By August Edward was at Rhuddlan with 750 horse, 8,000 foot and 1,000 archers, his progress along the coast had not been hampered. Ships from the Cinque ports were loaded with archers and crossbowmen and Anglesey was again taken by sea. In September Luke de Tany, one of Edward's household, was despatched to take command. By

Uchelwr c.1280 —

A man of some substance in 13th century Wales, the Uchelwr (nobleman) is wearing a red and yellow linen tabard with lions in reverse colours in each quarter. It was worn to keep the weather (both rain and direct sunlight) off the mail and emblazoned with armorial bearings to announce either the wearer's name or that of the man to whom he had sworn loyalty, in this case Llywelyn ap Gruffudd. A heavily decorated belt holds all in place. Well made leather pouches hang from the belt. Below the tabard the Uchelwr is wearing a fine linen crys (under-shirt) over which there is a padded, short sleeved jacket to allow for the free movement of the arms. A hauberk of mail is worn over this as a final protective layer, again short sleeved for ease of movement. He wears lined woollen trousers and riding boots. On his head is a coif of mail which protects him from cuts, especially around the throat, and a hood, again to provide protection from the elements. The helm being carried is a 'great helm' designed for knightly combat, which, although it may look impressive, was not favoured by many Uchelwyr.Despite appearances to contrary, this figure is not wearing a great deal of armour giving him an advantage of both speed and manoeuvrability.

The sword could be new or inherited, and has a straight cross bar and disc pommel. The sword belt is of soft leather and held in a bow across the hips at the most convenient angle to draw the blade. A knife is worn at the back as a secondary weapon. A mail glove is worn to protect the sword hand.

The cross hanging from his neck is worn as a symbol of faith.

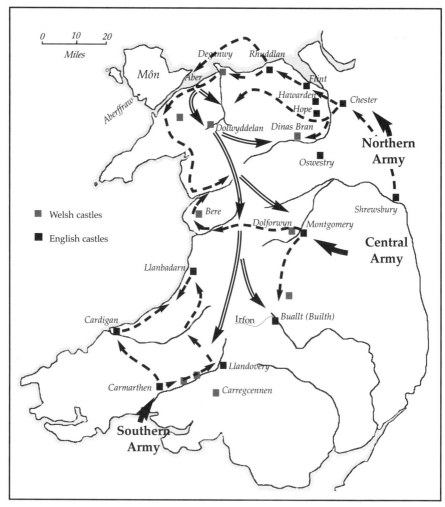

Wales: Second War of Independence, 1282–83

early November a pontoon bridge had been constructed across the straits to Bangor, and the outflanking of Llywelyn's positions was achieved.

Matters had not proceeded to plan in the south where there had been heavy fighting. The Welsh lords were not as willing to capitulate as they had been in 1276, and in June Gilbert de Clare had been defeated in ambush. In October Roger Mortimer died of natural causes and the Marcher forces were robbed of their leadership. Nevertheless by November the three armies had succeeded in pinning Llywelyn into Snowdonia. There was a brief pause in the fighting as Archbishop Pecham of Canterbury unsuccessfully attempted to negotiate a peace. Llywelyn and Dafydd would not yield to the king's demand to surrender the principality, and during the truce Luke de Tany ignored his orders by crossing the Menai and attempted to establish himself on the mainland. His army was ambushed as it crossed the bridge and in the ensuing rout Luke and sixteen household knights were killed.

This disaster broke the ring of armies around Snowdonia and allowed Llywelyn a chance to escape, and, whilst Edward summoned reinforcements for a protracted winter campaign, Llywelyn moved rapidly south to rally support in the middle March. To these ends he was in the vicinity of Builth on 11 December when his army was attacked by a force led by the Marcher Lord Roger Lestrange at Orewin bridge. Separated from the main body of his host, Llywelyn was killed by Stephen de Frankton of Shropshire. Edward was notified of the death of the prince of Wales in a letter from Roger Lestrange written immediately following the battle:

Cilmeri, near Builth, the memorial to Llywelyn ap Gruffudd.

Inform the king that the troops under Roger's command fought with Llywelyn ap Gruffydd in the land of Buellt on Friday next after the feast of St. Nicholas, that Llywelyn ap Gruffydd is dead, his army defeated, and all the flower of his army dead, as the bearer of this letter will tell.[21]

The death of Prince Llywelyn did not end the war. Dafydd was still at large, and Edward was keen to have him taken and the matter ended. By January reinforcements were gathered and Edward marched inland from Rhuddlan to Betws-y-Coed, taking Dolwyddelan castle. Plans were made for a campaign in mid Wales, and writs were issued to nine earls and seventy seven magnates to muster at Montgomery in May.[22] They were not to be needed, as on 25 April the last Welsh stronghold, Castell-y-Bere fell. Dafydd remained at large until 21 June when he was finally handed over to royal troops.

Wales was conquered and Edward's attention was turned to consolidating his gains. Much of the captured territory was given to lords faithful in their service to the crown. Anglesey, Gwynedd west of the Conwy, Flintshire, Carmarthen and Cardigan were retained as royal lordships. The Statute of Rhuddlan was enacted in 1284 to administer these districts, while the rest effectively became marcher lordships, such as southern Powys, still ruled by Gruffudd ap Gwenwynwyn, who had remained loyal to the crown throughout the war. As in 1277 castles were constructed to subjugate the defeated Welsh; Conwy, Caernarfon and Harlech the greatest amongst them.

Though Wales was conquered it was still to remain a problem for the rest of the century. Rhys ap Maredudd of Dryslwyn had remained loyal to the crown in 1282, hoping to receive the castle of Dinefwr, the traditional capital of Deheubarth as his reward. He did not receive the castle, however, which was retained in royal hands. Rhys was angered by the treatment he had received at the hands of the crown, and on 8 June 1287 he rebelled. Dinefwr, Carreg Cennan and Llandovery castles fell, and he ravaged as far as Swansea, Aberystwyth and Brecon. Edward was absent from England, but his brother and regent Earl Edmund of Cornwall was equal to the task of quashing the rebels. By the middle of August he had 10,600 foot and 600 horse ready for the siege of Dryslwyn, and the Marchers had raised a combined force of a further 12,500. Many of the troops were drawn from Wales, and all were marshalled as paid forces quickly and efficiently.[23] Dryslwyn fell in September and all was restored to order, though Rhys rebelled again in November and took Emlyn castle. It was besieged and taken in January 1288, though Rhys escaped and lived as a fugitive until 1292 when he was captured and hanged.

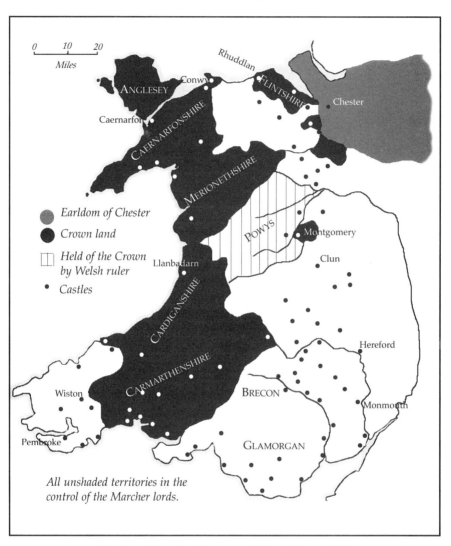

Wales: After the Statute of Rhuddlan, 1284

Rhys' rebellion had been local in nature and was quickly dealt with, so that it did not present a threat to the order of the realm. The rebellion of 1294 was more widespread and dangerous. The leaders of this rebellion were scattered across Wales, the foremost of them being Madog ap Llywelyn in the north. The rebellion began on 30 September, as Welsh troops were summoned to serve in a royal army on the continent. Cardigan, Builth, Bere, Denbigh and Caernarfon were all stormed and taken, but within a few weeks, despite the number of troops already overseas, Edward had raised some 31,000 foot and 250 knights at Chester, Montgomery and Gloucester.[24]

By Christmas Edward had marched to Conwy, having first reduced Perfeddwlad. A drive to Bangor in January was turned back when in an ambush the Welsh were able to take his baggage, and Edward returned to Conwy, abandoning his intended winter campaign. The castles of Aberystwyth, Harlech and Cricieth, cut off from England, were resupplied by sea throughout the winter. In February 1295 Madoc pushed into Powys and on the night of 5 March was brought to battle at Maes Moydog by William Beauchamp, earl of Warwick. Madoc himself escaped as his spearmen were first broken by archers and crossbowmen and then ridden down and smashed by heavy cavalry. In April Edward moved to Bangor, and then spent several weeks touring Wales reducing opposition. By August he was in Westminster having come to terms with Madoc, and Wales was, at last, secure.

Notes

1. J. E. Lloyd, *A history of Wales*, v.II, London, Longmans, 1912, p.427.
2. J. Beeler, *Warfare in England 1066–1189*, Ithaca, Cornell University Press, 1966, p.221.
3. J Beeler, *Warfare in England 1066–1189*, Ithaca, Cornell University Press, 1966, p.222.
4. J. Beeler, *Warfare in England 1066–1189*, Ithaca, Cornell University Press, 1966, p.224.
5. *Brut y Tywysogion*, p.42.
6. J. Beeler, *Warfare in England 1066–1189*, Ithaca, Cornell University Press, 1966, p.231.
7. J. E Lloyd, *A history of Wales*, v.II, London, Longmans, 1912, pp. 470–71.
8. Brut y Tywysogion, p.51.
9. J. Beeler, *Warfare in England 1066-1189*, Ithaca, Cornell University Press, 1966, p.236.
10. J. Beeler, *Warfare in England 1066-1189*, Ithaca, Cornell University Press, 1966, pp.242–44.

11. J. Beeler, *Warfare in England 1066-1189*, Ithaca, Cornell University Press, 1966, pp.254–55.

12. J. E. Lloyd, *A history of Wales*, vII, London, Longmans, 1912, pp. 634–35.

13. J. E. Lloyd, *A history of Wales*, v.II, London, Longmans, 1912, p. 639.

14. T. Matthews, (ed.) *Welsh records in Paris*, Carmarthen, W. Spurrell and Son, 1910, p.57.

15. J. E. Lloyd, *A history of Wales,* v.II, London, Longmans,1912, pp.647–49.

16. J. G. Edwards, *Littere Wallie*, Cardiff, University of Wales Press, 1940, p.xxxviii.

17. M. Powicke, *The thirteenth century 1216–1307*, Oxford, Oxford University Press, 1953, p.401.

18. R. R. Davies, *The age of Conquest. Wales 1063–1415*, Oxford, Oxford University Press, 1992, p.358.

19. D. Stephenson, 'Llywelyn ap Gruffydd and the struggle for the principality of Wales, 1258–1282', *Transactions of the honourable society of Cymmrodorion*, 1983, p. 44.

20. M. Prestwich, *Edward I*, London, Methuen, 1988, p.182.

21. J. G. Edwards, (ed.) *Calendar of Ancient Correspondence concerning Wales*, Cardiff, University of Wales Press, 1935, pp.83-84.

22. M. Prestwich, *Edward I*, London, Methuen, 1988, p.195.

23. M. Powicke, *The thirteenth century. 1216–1307*, Oxford, Oxford University Press, 1953, pp.439-40.

24. M Powicke, *The thirteenth century. 1216–1307*, Oxford, Oxford University Press, 1253, pp.441–43.

Chapter 5
Strategy and Logistics

The overlying theme of relations between England and Wales from 1100-1250 was one of a constant drive to implement overlordship on the part of the English, and Welsh efforts to throw off the Norman yoke. Although the Welsh became better at fighting them off, the Normans became better at raising armies and when favoured by circumstances royal campaigns could have spectacular results. The Treaty of Woodstock was a victory unparalleled by any other English king: 'Henry III's victory in 1246–7 was more thorough and comprehensive — for it extended to every part of native Wales, not merely to Gwynedd — than that achieved by any earlier king of England in Wales.'[1] Henry's position though was to be eroded, and by 1267 Llywelyn ap Gruffudd had achieved a position never before attained by a Welsh prince. The policy Edward I pursued therefore was different to those of previous monarchs. He first attempted to accept the dominance of Gwynedd, but then destroyed it, restoring the status-quo. The war of 1282 was to force Edward into a policy never before followed by the crown, the conquest of native Wales.

The major reason why the Anglo-Normans were not ejected from Wales during the numerous Welsh offensives throughout these two centuries was their extensive use of castles: 'The castle was the key to Norman success.'[2] Castles enabled the Normans to hold on during the rebellions and to reconquer afterwards. Castles allowed the Normans to hold down their territories with small armies, and it was the sheer number of castles which often balked Welsh counter offensives,

> A Welsh leader might deal effectively with one castle, or even three or four major centres. But the large network of castles scattered throughout the marches meant that no leader could penetrate the defence in depth and maintain heavy pressure on the Normans over a wide front.'[3]

Castles fell and lordships were taken, especially as the Welsh became better versed in siege tactics, but even in the combined offensives which sometimes happened, the Welsh could not muster enough troops to invest every castle in the marches. Thus the Anglo-Normans were able to retain footholds, and gradually expand again after the Welsh were spent.

The period in general was one of consolidation along the marches. Created by war in the eleventh century, they needed to be vigorously defended against the resurgent Welsh lords. It was a period of intensive castle building, old sites being upgraded and new ones constructed in the latest styles of stone: 'The defence of the march was underpinned by military strength.'[4] Limited as far as expansion was concerned, the Marchers extended their authority within their lordships. For example, the Clares of Glamorgan acquired the earldom in 1217 and from then on pressured the lords of the upland commotes into submission. This ongoing process culminated in 1267 with the removal of Gruffudd ap Rhys of Senghennydd, and the construction of Caerphilly castle. The jurisdictional range of Cardiff was also extended to cover the whole lordship.

Henry I was to an extent lucky when he became king, for he had a free hand within the Marches. All three earldoms were in his hands, Hereford and Shrewsbury by forfeiture and Chester by wardship, as Earl Hugh died in 1101 and his heir was a minor. Therefore across the entire march the crown had a direct hand in border affairs, and Henry could install whom he desired. The removal of Robert de Belleme and his brother Arnulf de

Montgomery, lord of Pembroke left a vacuum into which lesser families could filter. One of the first benefactors was Arnulfs castellan of Pembroke, Gerald of Windsor, who soon became a major figure in the south. Carmarthen was quickly established as a royal centre. All this was lost in the reign of Stephen, Carmarthen being captured by the Welsh, but this does not detract from Henry I's achievement. He created lordships from which his power radiated. He granted, resumed and regranted lordships in such a way that every lord, Welsh or Marcher, depended upon him as absolute overlord.

An example of Henry's overlordship can be seen in his dealings with Cadwgan ap Bleddyn of Ceredigion. In 1109 he was stripped of his lands, but after swearing homage to Henry, he was allowed to redeem them on strict conditions for the sum of £100.[5] In 1110 Cadwgan's son Owain murdered William of Brabant, a leading Fleming of the district, and as a result Henry deposed Cadwgan, donating his lands to Gilbert Fitz Richard de Clare.

That Henry I did not attempt to conquer Wales but merely control it is clear. Natives such as Cadwgan were only removed if they failed to toe the line and maintain stability. Hostages and tributes were frequently demanded, and Henry also considered the Welsh to be judicially answerable to him. Formal submissions were exacted as graphic illustrations of overlordship, as the entry in the Anglo-Saxon chronicle for 1114 states: 'The Welsh kings came to him and became his vassals and swore oaths of allegiance to him.[6]

The ultimate tool to impose authority was the royal campaign, but as Henry I only needed to lead two, it is clear that his authority was seldom seriously challenged. The most peaceful times between England and Wales were those when the crown succeeded in creating a personal relationship with a prominent Welsh magnate. Henry I's reign was one such period, as was the first decade of John's, when he and Llywelyn ab Iorwerth enjoyed cordial relations. The most startling example though can be seen in the reign of Henry II. For the first decade he attempted to subjugate the Welsh with campaign after campaign, resulting in nothing but a waste of time and money. One of the reasons for this offensive policy may have been an effort to repay the marcher lords for the aid they gave him against Stephen. Now he attempted to wrest from the Welsh the territories which had been lost. Certainly he was not attempting conquest, but a return to the stability and status-quo of Henry I's reign. Military force was not going to achieve this, and after 1165 he tried a different tactic.

This change of plan can be seen as just that, a change in tactics but not in the overall goal. The attempt at achieving stability through conciliation worked, and between them Henry and the Lord Rhys were successful in keeping Wales more or less stable until the former's death in 1189. A further reason for Henry's change of tactics may well lie in that south Wales made an excellent embarkation point for Ireland, and Henry was anxiously casting an eye in that direction during the 1160s and 1170s.

The Anglo-Norman invasion of Ireland and the creation of lordships there did not meet with his approval, and he was keen to go to Ireland himself to curb his adventurous lords and bring them back under his authority. The invasion of Ireland can be seen as important for three reasons: it acted as a spur towards Rhys and Henry reaching an agreement; it removed several of Rhys' enemies and therefore facilitated his rise to preeminence, and more importantly, it finally cut off the supply of Viking mercenaries and ships, closing a safe haven that the Welsh had relied upon many times before.

Richard, John and Henry III can all be seen to follow a similar policy, a refusal to allow the lords of Wales to gain the ascendancy. Richard and John pursued an aggressive policy which ultimately can be seen to be unsuccessful, in that by John's death Llywelyn ab Iorwerth was undisputedly master of Wales. Henry III followed a more sedate strategy, acknowledging Llywelyns' supremacy, but refusing to recognise it with a treaty. His prompt action to curb Gwynedd under Dafydd shows this, but again it can ultimately be seen to have been unsuccessful, for it was Henry III who granted to Llywelyn ap Gruffudd the Treaty of Montgomery. All three kings discovered that as long as they were pre-occupied with external issues, they did not have the power to curb the lords of Wales, who were masters at exploiting royal weakness.

Edward I's campaign of 1276 was intended to bring a recalcitrant vassal to heel; his second to crush him and conquer Wales once and for all. All of Edward's actions in Wales followed a common strategy, whatever their ultimate aim was at the time, establishing three commands covering north, central and south Wales, with commanders given independent action within the overall plan. The Welsh attempted their tactics of ambush to resist, and enjoyed some success, for example the defeats of Gilbert de Clare and Luke de Tany in 1282.

They can also be seen to use a wider common strategy, as numerous local risings forced the king to raise large numbers of troops, and denied him the luxury of concentrating them all into one force. This can be seen in the rebellions of 1282 and 1294. A further common theme can be distinguished in that both of these wars were fought as mobile campaigns, which were intended to deny the English the ability to surround and destroy them. Unfortunately Llywelyn's break out from Snowdonia and Madog's push into Powys both ended in disaster when the English were able to catch them. 'The second war, like the first, had been won not by brilliant feats of generalship or decisive battles but by the efficient garnering and intelligent deployment of resources.'[7] This can also be seen in the defeat of the two post-conquest rebellions. The English had the resources to raise several large armies and the discipline to methodically advance and entrap the enemy, thereby rendering the Welsh strategy irrelevant.

Throughout these centuries the knight remained the spine of royal armies. About 180 lay tenants, all the bishoprics in England apart from Carlisle, and many monasteries all owed knights to the crown. This would yield in total some 5,000–6,000.[8] The core of an army would be a contingent of household troops. In Henry III's reign the household consisted of 100 or more knights, a similar number of mounted sergeants and a large number of foot sergeants and archers. These would for the most part serve in garrisons, but on campaign could provide an advance guard, headquarters staff, battlefield commanders or an elite brigade.[9] It appears that in the twelfth century knights, at least of the household, were organised into units of ten called constabularia, or multiples thereof. In 1176 William Fitz Aldelin was sent to Ireland at the head of ten knights, as was John de Courcy. Similarly, Robert Fitz Stephen and Miles de Cogan were sent with twenty. This system of organisation seems to have broken down during the thirteenth century, and the cavalry came to be more loosely organised on the individual retinues.[10]

The equipment used by a knight gradually changed over the period. The major component of armour remained the mail hauberk, sometimes fitted with integral coifs to cover the head, and usually extended to the wrists, often with attached mittens. From the middle of the twelfth century mail leggings came to be used. A knight did not need a large kite shield to protect his legs any more, and consequently shields were reduced in size, becoming the roughly triangular heater shields. Helmets became more elaborate, the simple nasal developing into face plates. Sides were added until the great helm was developed. Worn over a padded skull cap, it covered the entire head with thin slits left for vision and breathing. Although affording good protection these helmets cut vision and hearing to a minimum, making communication in battle extremely difficult.

During the thirteenth century armour came to be supplemented with plates, either of iron or cuirbouilli, boiled rigid leather. First added to the knees, shins and lower arms, by 1300 a knight's limbs could be covered with plate defences over his mail. Between the heraldic surcoat and the hauberk might be a coat of plates: a leather tunic on to which overlapping metal plates were riveted. This would provide an extra, semi-rigid layer of defence against crushing weapons.[11]

Weapons themselves also developed as time passed. The lance became longer and heavier, often twelve or fourteen feet long, it could only be used couched. Swords also became longer and heavier, some types developing into stabbing rather than cutting weapons as armour improved. As earlier, lances and swords continued to be supplemented with other weapons, such as maces, hammers and axes.[12]

Knights were not the only cavalry to be found on a battlefield. These centuries saw the use in Shropshire of men called muntatores. They seem to have been sub-knightly, holding half a knight's fee. Armed with hauberk, light helmet and lance, they rode light horses and seem to have been light cavalry and mounted infantry who served in castle garrisons and on campaign against the Welsh, usually for a term of forty days. Though the term muntator is almost exclusively from Shropshire, similar troops served in similar ways along the entire border.[13] Companies of light horse were used to fight off and pursue Welsh

English knight, late 13th C
© *The Board of Trustees of the Armouries*
The mail hauberk now extends to the wrist with detachable mitten gauntlets. Legs and feet are protected by chausses, mail stockings. The head is protected by a great helm and mail coif, under which would be a considerable amount of padding. Over the mail, and hidden by the surcoat, is a coat of plates, a semi-rigid layer made up of metal plates riveted to a fabric base. The shield, which no longer needs to be large, has shrunk to a handier size. The lance is now longer and can only be used couched. Great Welsh lords, such as Llywelyn ap Gruffudd and his retainers, may also have looked like this, whilst English light horse probably resembled the earlier Norman cavalry.

raiders, and to act as scouts and skirmishers on campaign.

Mercenaries continued to form an important part of English armies in the twelfth century, although with less internal strife during the thirteenth, their use was infrequent. During the early twelfth century the use of the fyrd died out, replaced by taxes to pay for more professional, better armed and trained mercenaries. Scutage paid to avoid campaigning could also be used to hire mercenary troops who were frequently better quality and often more loyal than feudal forces. Increasingly mercenary knights and foot came to fill the ranks alongside feudal levies, and it was not just the crown which enjoyed their services. In his rebellion of 1102 Robert de Belleme's best troops at Bridgenorth were his mercenaries.[14]

Infantry could be mercenary or feudal, sergeants sworn to serve as footmen or commoners making up the levy. The obligation of every freeman to serve in arms was reaffirmed by Henry II's Assize of arms in 1181. It stipulated the kind of equipment every freeman was to own according to wealth, ranging from a hauberk, helmet, lance and shield for those holding a knight's fee, down to a gambeson, helmet and lance for the poorer commoners. These forces were raised by sheriffs and were paid and provisioned by the king. Infantry were organised into basic units of twenty commanded by a vintenar, and then into hundreds under a constable. This was shown in 1193 by the recruitment of 500 Welshmen, 25 of whom were officers.[15]

A major innovation made by Edward I was the use of commissions of array. In 1277 sheriffs were ordered to bring specific numbers of troops, but in 1282 household knights were sent out recruit men from given areas. This method did not guarantee the quality of the levies, as corruption at any level might yield only a large number of ill equipped and inept men, rather than good ones.[16] The number of archers within the ranks of the infantry steadily increased as Edward's reign passed, and even by the second war the majority of foot were archers. If the accounts of the battles of Orewin Bridge and Maes Moydog are to be believed, then we can also see emerging in the English armies the tactic of setting the archers 'Interlaced with the heavy cavalry,' which was to smash William Wallace at Falkirk and become the standard tactic of English armies.[17] Much use was made of troops from south Wales and the Marches, who were frequently recruited in a similar way to native service.

How the Welsh raised their forces is not known with any certainty. Though Llywelyn ap Gruffudd could call upon heavy cavalry, whether they could be termed knights in any but a strictly military sense is unknown. If these troops served as a feudal obligation, no records of their tenure survive. It is likely that the core of the prince's army was his teulu, as it always had been. To this he could add the warbands of lords who served him on campaign and any other levies which were mustered. There were professional soldiers in the army by now, as Llywelyn had both castles and a siege train, but whether these troops would be members of a teulu, or some new force is unknown.

The military service imposed on Gwynedd by the Crown in 1247 can be seen to have been of a similar nature to Welsh modes. Llywelyn and Owain had to supply 24 knights and 1000 footmen at their own expense for service in Wales, and 500 foot at crown expense for service in England. Either Llywelyn, Owain or one of their heirs was expected to lead the levy.[18] Although it is true that troops were only expected to serve for six weeks on an external campaign under the Welsh princes and Henry III did not specify the length of service, the two modes were otherwise the same.[19]

Cavalry were raised as paid or feudal contingents. In 1277 the feudal host was summoned to Worcester, and paid forces were also gathered and placed under the command of household knights. Along with the shire levies woodsmen, diggers and engineers were called upon from the counties. Supplies were gathered and stored at central bases. Three centres of operation were established under William Beauchamp at Chester, Roger Mortimer at Shrewsbury, and Payn de Chaworth at Carmarthen. The feudal muster raised 228 knights and 294 sergeants, but this was not the whole cavalry force. Others served for pay whilst others performed their service voluntarily at their own expense. In all there was probably 800 cavalry in the main army, and by the time it had reached Rhuddlan, nearly 16,000 foot, 9000 of which were Welsh.[20] All the mechanisms available to a thirteenth century general were employed to raise and manage the armies, to the extent that, 'It is probable that this army was the best controlled, as it was the best led, that had been gathered in Britain since the Norman conquest.'[21]

The campaign of 1282 was hastily organised but still thorough in preparation. Three days after Hawarden fell the commands were established, and soon after household knights were despatched, Amadeus of Savoy leading a relief force towards Rhuddlan as early as April 7th. Writs for a muster of magnates to take paid service by 17 May were issued, and by the end of the month over 200 cavalry were in royal pay.[22] Following this muster a second, for feudal service, was made for troops to meet at Rhuddlan on August 2nd. This feudal summons raised 123 knights and 190 sergeants. Among this contingent were many of the earls, for none of them served for pay. They and their retinues did feudal or voluntary service. From all his sources, Edward probably had 800 cavalry.[23]

The campaigns launched by Hubert de Burgh, though achieving little militarily, nevertheless show that the crown could put large forces into the field. In the 1228 campaign 425 feudal and 120 household knights served with the king.[24] Maintaining such forces in the field and keeping them supplied was still a difficult task, as was shown in the campaign of 1231. A force of 600 knights was gathered, and 1,000 axemen levied from ten counties. The infantry contingent is not known but we can assume that it too was large. Merchants were expected to bring supplies to the army, and markets along the border were suspended. Sheriffs were to ensure that their levies were supplied for an initial forty day period. However, merchants did not arrive and many of the levies were not provisioned. The army was too large for the few supplies that it received, and reinforcements had to be sent home.

The processes of supplying armies improved under Edward I. In 1282 a permanent supply base was established at Chester and filled with 23,000 quarters of grain. 11,000 cattle and 6,600 tuns of wine were also collected.[25] Carts were requisitioned from monasteries, and much use was made of the royal right of prise: the compulsory purchase of goods at cost. Supplies were collected by clerks and sheriffs from given areas under writ. Trade with Wales was sanctioned and markets along the border suspended to compel merchants to come to the armies. Ireland, Gasconny and Ponthieu were all called upon to send victuals, and some magnates made their own provisions for supplying their retinues. The seizure of the grain from Anglesey must also have aided the situation a great deal. The campaign of 1282–83 cost £60,000 excluding castle building, proof of the huge undertaking the conquest had been.

The writer of the Brut y Tywysogyon mentions the last movements and events of the life of Llywelyn ap Gruffudd in a very matter of fact way.[26] It is hardly surprising that the account is reticent and lacking detail, for the battle of Orewin bridge marked the end of an era. Wales was conquered, its independence ended. There were rebellions to follow, but such was Edward I's grip on Wales that it could not be shaken off. After over two hundred years of almost continual fighting, royal dominance over Wales was permanently established. Ultimately, it had to be imposed through no mere claim of overlordship and a treaty with a dominant figure, but the removal of such figures and outright conquest by a strong monarch, who was not distracted by internal difficulties within the rest of his domains.

Notes

1. R. R. Davies, *The age of conquest. Wales 1063–1415*, Oxford, Oxford University Press, 1992, p.303.
2. D. Walker, *The Norman conquerors*, Swansea, Christopher Davies Publishers, 1977, p.56.
3. D. Walker, *The Norman conquerors*, Swansea, Christopher Davies Publishers, 1977, p.64.
4. R. R. Davies, *The age of conquest. Wales 1063–1415*, Oxford, Oxford University Press, 1992, p.281.
5. R. R. Davies, 'Henry I and Wales', in H. Mayr-Harting and R. I. Moore (eds) *Studies in mediaeval history presented to R. H. C. Davies*, London, Hambledon Press, 1985, p.140.
6. *Anglo-Saxon chronicle*, p.183.
7. I. Rowlands, 'The Edwardian conquest and its military consolidation', in T. Herbert and G. E. Jones, (eds.) *Edward I and Wales*, Cardiff, University of Wales Press, 1988, p.48.
8. J. Beeler *Warfare in England 1066–1189*, Ithaca, Cornell University Press, 1966, pp.265–66.
9. M. Powicke, *Military obligation in mediaeval England*, Oxford, Oxford University Press, pp.64–65.
10. M. Prestwich, *Armies and warfare in the middle ages. The English experience*, New Haven, Yale University Press, 1996, p.49.
11. C. Rothero, *The Scottish and Welsh wars 1250–1400*, London, Osprey, 1986, pp.20–21.
12. C. Rothero, *The Scottish and Welsh wars 1250–1400*, London, Osprey, 1986, p.22.
13. F. C. Suppe, *Military institutions on the Welsh marches*, Woodbridge, Boydell Press, 1994, p.74.
14. J. Beeler, *Warfare in England 1066–1189*, Ithaca, Cornell University Press, 1966, p.299.
15. M. Prestwich, *Armies and warfare in the middle ages. The English experience*, New Haven, Yale University Press, 1996, p.127.
16. M. Prestwich, *Armies and warfare in the middle ages. the English experience*, New Haven, Yale University Press, 1996, pp.123–24.
17. M. Powicke, *The thirteenth century. 1216–1307*, Oxford, Oxford University Press, 1953, p.428.
18. C. W. Lewis, 'The treaty of Woodstock 1247, its background and significance', *Welsh history review* 2, 1964, p.47.
19. C. W. Lewis, 'The Treaty of Woodstock 1247, its background and significance', *Welsh history review* 2, 1964, pp.61–64.
20. M. Prestwich, *Edward I*, London, Methuen, 1988, pp.179–80.
21. M. Powicke, *The thirteenth century, 1216–1307*, Oxford, Oxford University Press, 1953, p.411.
22. M. Prestwich, *Edward I*, London, Methuen, 1988, p.189.

23. M. Prestwich, *Edward I*, London, Methuen, 1988, p.197.

24. R. F. Walker, 'Hubert de Burgh and Wales 1218–1232' , *English historical review* 87, 1972, p.480.

25. M. Prestwich, *Armies and warfare in the middle ages. the English experience*, New Haven, Yale University Press, 1996, p.251.

26. *Brut y Tywysogion*, pp.120–21.

Chapter 6
Castles

The use of castles by the crown and the lords of the march in their efforts to subjugate the Welsh has already been discussed in previous chapters, but it is necessary to examine this strategy in more detail. Castles first appeared along the Welsh border before the conquest of England, the residences of Earl Ralph of Hereford and his followers. As the Normans began their incursions into Welsh territory following the conquest, they naturally brought their castle building strategy with them, and before long there were many castles along the border and in the captured territory. Any study of Anglo-Welsh warfare should, therefore, examine both the use and military development of the castle.

Most early castles began their lives as structures of timber and earth, the most common being the motte-and-bailey. Robert of Rhuddlan's castle was one such, for example. These castles were of two parts, foremost of which was the motte. It was an artificial or enlarged natural mound of earth surrounded with a ditch and surmounted by a wooden palisade and tower. The tower could be quite elaborate, and served as the residence for the owner and a last line of defence. The second part of the castle, the bailey, was an enclosure surrounded by a ditch and palisade, within which were placed the hall and other buildings for acommodation and storage. Some castles might have two or more baileys, depending upon the size and number of ancillary buildings. Generally these enclosures would follow any contours or features of the land upon which they were built, and consequently are irregular or curvilinear in shape.

The entrance to the bailey was usually guarded by a tower, sometimes constructed of stone, and the two parts of the castle were joined by wing walls up the motte. Access between the two parts was provided by either a

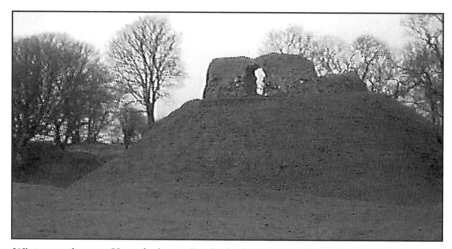

Wiston castle, near Haverfordwest, Pembrokeshire — possibly the best example of a motte and bailey castle in Wales, which was built in the early 12th century and destroyed by Llywelyn ap Iorwerth in 1220.

flight of steps or a flying bridge of timber, as at Hen Domen castle, the original Montgomery.[1] These bridges could be broken down to deny an enemy who had captured the bailey an easy route up the motte. The other form of earthwork castle was the ringwork. Here, the motte was replaced by an enclosure protected by earth ramparts, effectively another bailey which had stronger defences.

The main benefit of these castles was that they were quick to establish and did not require a skilled workforce, a small number of carpenters and many diggers would suffice. They were also relatively cheap to build, earth and timber being abundant natural resources in most areas. However quick and cheap to build initially, some motte-and-baileys became very elaborate constructions as time went on, and their defences could be very strong. Hen Domen never became a stone castle, though it had a long life, and in its final form it was nevertheless a powerful fortress. Double rows of post holes along the earth banks denote that they were crowned with a double palisade, the outer higher than the inner, the space between filled with earth to create a box rampart with a protected walk-way along the top. Large timber towers jutted forwards from these ramparts, overlooking a deep and wide ditch. Storming these defences would be a formidable task.[2]

Not all motte-and-bailey castles were intended to be permanent sites though. Some therefore had a short life, such as Bromlow and Lady House in the vale of Montgomery. This factor enables the progress of the Norman advance to be followed, as one site was abandoned for a new one further westwards. In some cases, as in the vale of Montgomery, a typological study of each motte can show how many individual lords were involved in the process of advance.[3]

The most obvious weakness of a timber castle, other than the natural tendency of wood to rot and require constant replacing, was its vulnerability to fire. The best way to circumvent this danger was to replace timber with stone whenever time and circumstances permitted. Some castles were built of stone from the beginning. Chepstow castle was established and built by William fitz Osbern before his death in 1071, and it took the form of a two story hall with a stone curtain wall surrounding it. It is likely that Chepstow was the first stone castle to be built in Britain.[4] Ludlow was another masonry castle which was established before the end of the eleventh century.

Early transitions into stone often took the form of a direct exchange of timber for masonry. If the motte was a natural feature, or if enough time had passed for it to consolidate sufficiently, the palisade which crowned it could

Chepstow castle, the first castle to be built in stone by the Normans (the work was commenced by William fitz Osbern in about 1067). Overlooking the river Wye, Chepstow was expanded in the 12th and 13th centuries.

be replaced in stone creating a shell-keep with a defended wall walk along its top and buildings abutted to the inner face. Cardiff castle has a keep of this type. Alternatively the whole of the motte could be cleared and a stone tower built upon it, or, as was more common, the motte was abandoned and replaced by a tower-keep. These huge buildings relied for defence upon the passive strength of their immensely thick walls, and contained all the rooms the lord of the castle required for his residence. The defences of the bailey were also replaced by stone walls which followed the line of the initial ramparts.

Further developments in castle design were introduced during the second half of the twelfth century, pioneered in England by Henry II.[5] The first fundamental change came with reconstructing curtain walls in straight sections with protruding towers at each angle. This broke the wall up into open faced sections which could be swept by archers shooting through arrow loops within the mural towers, and therefore protected from return fire. This change of plan shifted the entire strategy of castle defence from passive to offensive, actively attacking the enemy while remaining in safety. Such changes as this were caused by developments in weapon technology.

Bronllys castle, built in c.1200 is a single circular keep built on an earlier earth motte.

The creation of mural towers and straight walls were directly related to the growing use of the crossbow. Inter-linked fields of fire across the wall faces were a stiff deterrent to attacking forces. Improvements in siege weaponry brought further developments to castle design. Sharp angles were vulnerable to picks and undermining, and so shapes other than rectangular were experimented with for towers and keeps. In 1189 William Marshall became earl of Pembroke upon marrying the heiress Isabella de Clare. He rebuilt Pembroke castle with round flanking towers, a strong curtain wall and a massive round keep, pierced on it's upper three levels with many arrow loops.[6] Round keeps, though not common, had a long life, as Cefnllys was rebuilt with a round keep by Roger Mortimer in 1173–74. Bronllys and Skenfrith also had round keeps, and even the castle of Flint, begun in 1277 was constructed with a round keep.

The introduction in about 1200 of the trebuchet, a stone throwing artillery piece of massive power, caused the building of curtain walls much thicker and higher than before. Gates were also improved, making this naturally weak point in the circuit of defence stronger. Often the gate was placed between a pair of flanking towers, elongated to create a passage, and joined over the gate to provide lodgings and guard positions. These passages would contain numerous gates and portcullises, and arrow loops from the sides and murder holes in the roof of the passage would allow defenders to harry any attackers within. So large and strong did these gatehouses become that they frequently took over the role of the keep which was now rendered obsolete, though not useless.[7]

The castle reached its ultimate form in the later thirteenth century with the development of concentric defences, pioneered by Gilbert de Clare at Caerphilly in Glamorgan, the greatest of all the marcher castles. In these castles, a low outer wall was dominated by a massive inner, with only a narrow strip between the two. All the buildings of the castle would be contained within the inner ward, and defenders upon both walls would be able to bring their combined firepower to bear upon attackers. Especially when combined with extensive water defences as at Caerphilly, these castles were all but impregnable. Caerphilly and Edward I's castle of Caernarfon only fell to assault in 1270 and 1294 respectively because they were unfinished at the time.

It is not surprising that there are more castles along the Welsh marches than anywhere else in Britain.[8] The pioneer of post-conquest castle building was William fitz Osbern. During his short reign as earl of Hereford he created a system of castles along his western frontier, including Clifford, Ludlow and Wigmore.[9] The Marchers also established fortresses in the

Caerphilly, a superb concentric castle, (the second largest castle in Britain) was started by Gilbert de Clare in 1268 in response to the expansive policy being pursued by Llywelyn ap Gruffudd. It was destroyed by the latter in 1270 and rebuilding commenced almost immediately and the castle was complete by 1277.

Welsh lands which they invaded; Chepstow by 1071, Rhuddlan and Montgomery (Hen Domen) by 1086, Cardiff, Carmarthen and Pembroke by 1092 and Aberlleinog on Anglesey by 1094.

> The castle was the key to the Normans' success in maintaining a military presence in an invaded territory. Earth and timber fortifications could be set up in a short time to consolidate newly conquered lands, to guard strategic areas and act as bases for further operations.[10]

Castles did indeed act in this way. The castles of the Marchers enabled them to maintain foot holds in their territories during the risings of the end of the eleventh century, and throughout the twelfth and thirteenth. Without these secure bases it is likely that the Normans would have been utterly ejected from Wales. Thus castles served the purpose for which they were built. The Normans built many, for even when several fell it was unlikely that any Welsh lord had the resources to invest all the castles of his enemy and take them before relief arrived. They served as bastions of defence in hostile lands, centres of royal or lordly control of these lands, and as guarantees of the permanence of that lordship.

To these ends new castles were constantly being built, whenever territory was acquired or to strengthen current lordships during times of unrest.

Castles could fulfil functions other than defence, however. Settlements could grow up outside a castle merely to service it, or they could be positively encouraged by the lord, creating a borough if it was deemed expedient. Nor was it only royal and marcher castles which generated settlements, Welshpool grew up beside the principal fortress of southern Powys, and the castle of Dolforwyn was envisaged as having a borough when it was built in 1273. In all there were some fifty-eight towns in Wales connected to a castle.[11]

Yet castles were always initially emplaced to provide centres of defence and expansion, and as such needed a constant garrison. Methods needed to be devised to supply one. William fitz Osbern peopled his castles by promising rich rewards to all who served him, and was never short of knights, but this was not a very reliable system. The obligation of guard service was created to supply garrisons. The terms of service varied from place to place as the numbers of knights and sergeants available differed. For example, at Richmond the earls' 187 knights were all expected to serve for sixty days per annum. At Norwich the forty knights served in groups of ten for ninety days, while at Hastings knights served for one month three times a year.[12]

Strategically located royal and baronial castles were emplaced within large honours or castleries, and it was from these districts a castle drew its garrison, or the money to pay one. Carmarthen was established as a castlery where the local Welsh lords did service. Before the end of the twelfth century the practice of commuting guard service for cash had begun. These payments would be used to hire a small professional force to hold the castle, which would be augmented in times of trouble by those who were bound to do service there. This system would create bands of professionals at each castle who would be invaluable in wartime.[13] Mercenaries could also be used as garrison troops.

The entirety of the Shropshire March was broken into castleries in this manner, and the lordship of Clun provides a good example. All the places which were held of guard service to Clun were within about six miles of the castle, or if further afield then they were located on an old Roman road which was still in service.[14] There was no castle at Clun before the Welsh rising of 1094, and it is likely that it was built in response to it by the lord Picot de Say. Soon after the construction of the motte and two baileys, which were replaced in stone throughout the later twelfth and thirteenth centuries, tenants would be enfeoffed who were charged with providing guard service.[15]

The Welsh were fully aware of the importance of castles to the English.

Clun castle, Shropshire, a spectacular ruin. Probably built by Picot de Say as a motte with two baileys in the late 11th century. The stone keep was built during the twelfth and thirteenth centuries.

Dinas Bran castle, Llangollen, built by the princes of Powys in the 13th century, it was abandoned in favour of a new castle at Holt after 1284. Its dominant position on the site of an Iron Age hill fort gave it control of the Dee valley.

Their preferred tactic of assault on castles was a surprise attack or sudden storm of the defences, as at Aberystwyth and Hawarden in 1282 but throughout the centuries some lords did acquire a knowledge of siege tactics. Pembroke was unsuccessfully besieged in 1094, and according to the Brut y Tywysogyon in 1193, 'In that year the warband of Maelgwn ap Rhys manfully breached the castle of Ystrad Meurig with slings and catapults.'[16]

Similarly in 1231,

> That same Maelgwn and Owain ap Gruffydd and their men, and with them the lord Llywelyn's men, went a second time to the town of Cardigan; and they laid siege to the castle. And after a few days they breached it with catapults, till the garrison was forced to surrender the castle and to leave it.[17]

The Welsh did not just learn to assault castles, but to build them. As early as 1111 Cadwgan ap Bleddyn planned to build one at Welshpool.[18] A motte-and-bailey was built at Cymer by Uchtryd ap Edwin by 1116. Between then and 1233 Brut y Tywysogyon records the construction of some twenty-four earthwork castles by the Welsh, and it is possible that many more of the mottes in and around Wales could be Welsh in origin. Stone castles were also constructed by the greater lords of Wales; Dinas-Bran in northern Powys, Welshpool in southern Powys, Dinefwr, Dryslwyn and Carreg Cennen in Deheubarth. The majority of the stone castles were constructed by the two Llywelyns, who built several to consolidate their hold throughout their lands: Dolbadarn, Dolwyddelan, Cricieth, Castell-y-Bere and Dolforwyn amongst them. Dafydd ap Gruffudd began construction of a castle at Hope following 1277, but it was unfinished at the time of the war in 1282–1283.

It is not known who designed these castles, or even how they were built, though the labour service owed to the prince was doubtless used to provide manpower. Usually the castles of the Welsh are well sited, to take advantage of craggy outcrops, and to cover strategic locations such as the convergence of tracks and roads as at Dolwyddelan, or at the head of passes such as Tomen-y-Rhodwydd. Also, castles might be sited as much as a symbol as for strategic reasons. Dolforwyn was built close by, and as a direct threat to Gruffudd ap Gwenwynwyns' capital of Welshpool.

Generally their design was simple and unimposing, constructed of poor masonry. Keeps dominated and there was a lack of mural towers or scientifically designed curtain walls.[19] Keeps in these native castles were generally of two floors, and constructed of better masonry. Entrance was on the first floor by steps, possibly contained within a fore building. Battlements were reached by intra mural stairs within the thickness of the wall, as spiral stairs were not used. Dolbadarn is unusual in this, as it is both

Dinefwr castle, Llandeilo, the seat of the rulers of Deuheubarth, is located on a high crag overlooking the Tywi valley in Carmarthenshire. The ruins that can be seen today were built in the 12th century when the castle was the property of the Lord Rhys.It remained in use until the 16th century.

Dolbadarn castle, Llanberis. Built in the late 12th century, probably by Llywelyn ap Iorwerth, Dolbadarn stands guard at the western entrance of the Llanberis Pass. For over 20 years it was the prison of Owain, the brother of Llywelyn ap Gruffudd.

Dolwyddelan castle, overlooking the valley of the Lledr in Gwynedd, was built in the late 12th century, probably by Iorwerth ap Owain. It was abandoned in the 16th century and a roof and pseudo-battlements were added by the Victorians.

Dolforwyn castle, Newtown, Powys, built during the 13th century by Llywelyn ap Gruffudd as a direct challenge to the nearby castle at Montgomery. It was besieged by Edward I for fifteen days in 1277 and later destroyed by him.

Llandovery castle was built in the late 13th century on an existing motte and bailey site. Probably originally built by Richard Fitz Pons in about 1116 it was captured by the Welsh in 1162 and was held by them for over 100 years, falling to Edward I in1277 and Llywelyn ap Gruffudd in 1282. It was besieged by Owain Glyndwr in 1403.

three floors high and has a spiral stair. The keeps were either rectangular, apsidal, or round in shape.

The first Welsh rebellion of 1287 was in its entirety a series of attacks upon castles. Rhys ap Maredudd stormed the castles of Llandovery, Dinefwr and Carreg Cennen. The English response was rapid and effective; a successful siege of Dryslwyn forced Rhys' initial surrender in September 1287, and a second siege in January 1288 of Newcastle Emlyn brought about the end of his second attempt.[20] Welsh castles could not resist a determined English siege, and during the wars of 1276–1277 and 1282-1283 their holders often slighted them rather than allow them to fall into English hands. This was done at Dinas Bran in 1277 and at Hope in 1282.

The conquest of Wales in 1282–1283 created problems for the monarch who achieved it: 'The whole of Gwynedd had now to be subdued and securely riveted down with castles.'[21] Edward I's castle building in Wales began in 1277 with the construction of Aberystwyth, Builth, Flint and Rhuddlan, the latter two covering the coastal route from Chester into Gwynedd. Rhuddlan was intended to serve as a forward base for royal authority, administration and control, but following 1282 these functions were transferred to Caernarfon. All of Edward's new castles, which formed a defensive arc around Gwynedd, shared several features, most notably that they were all designed to be supplied by sea in the event of a siege (with the exception of Builth which lay inland). Edward had learned of the Welsh ability at siegecraft, and taken steps to nullify it. Both Aberystwyth and Harlech were relieved by sea during the rebellion of 1294–1295.

In 1278 the Savoyard architect Master James of St. George was despatched to Wales to supervise the construction of the new castles. In 1282–1287 he was called upon again, designing Conwy, Caernarfon and Harlech himself. It was also Master James who designed and supervised the initial construction of Beaumaris castle in 1295. This collection of castles stand as the greatest examples of military architecture of the thirteenth century. Rhuddlan and Aberystwyth are partly concentric in design, twin circuits of mutually supporting walls running for the majority of the way around each castle. Harlech and Beaumaris are both fully concentric and stand with Caerphilly as perfect examples of the style. Conwy and Caernarfon both occupy long narrow sites not conducive to building concentric rings of defence, but they make up for this by the size and power of their single walls. Caernarfon especially is massively strong, the high curtain flanked with mural towers, and with fighting galleries installed in the thickness of the walls. Caernarfon, the legendary birthplace of the Roman emperor Magnus Maximus, was intended to be the capital of royal Gwynedd, and its construction reflects this. The castle walls are made of banded masonry of two colours and the towers are polygonal in shape, clearly aping the Theodosian defences of Constantinople.[22]

Edward's castles were never intended to act merely as military bases. They

Flint castle was the first castle to be built by Edward I in north Wales. Work began in 1277 and finished in 1286. The Great Tower (right) was probably inspired by the Tour de Constance in Aigues-Mortes, France.

The mighty fortress at Caernarfon was built by Edward I between 1283 and 1330. It was intended as the administrative centre of north Wales. The striped masonry in the walls is said to have been inspired by the walls of Constantinople.

were intended to be centres of English influence and to this end each one was constructed with an associated borough. The boroughs were not there simply to service the castle, nor to promote trade, but to impose Englishness upon the Welsh. They excluded all Welsh from within their walls and the burgesses who lived there were given considerable privileges.

The difficulty and cost of collecting together all the necessary masons, carpenters and other labourers required to build several large castles simultaneously was enormous. The native princes would never have been able to achieve it. Ultimately the resources of Edward I's England were only just able to cope. The cost came to some £93,000.[23] The value of this programme has been questioned, as the money might have been better spent in other ways.[24] Perhaps the sheer scale of the programme was excessive, but there was clear logic and tradition behind the strategy. Many times in the past castles had been built in Welsh lands, and many times they had proven their worth by holding out against Welsh attacks, allowing the English to regain the ascendancy. Edward I saw no reason to deviate from a strategy which by and large had enabled the Normans to retain a hold on Wales for the past two hundred years.

Notes

1. D. J. C. King, *The castle in England and Wales*, London, Routledge, 1991, p.56.
2. M. W. Thompson, *The rise of the castle*, Cambridge, Cambridge University Press, 1991, p.86.
3. D. J. C. King, and C. J. Spurgeon, 'The mottes of the vale of Montgomery', *Archaeologica Cambrensis* 114, 1965, pp.85–86.
4. M. W. Thompson, *The rise of the castle*, Cambridge, Cambridge University Press, 1991, p.73.
5. D. J. C. King, *The castle in England and Wales*, London, Routledge, 1991, p.91.
6. D. J. C. King, *The castle in England and Wales*, London, Routledge, 1991, pp.100 –101.
7. D. J. C. King, *The castle in England and Wales*, London, Routledge, 1991, pp.118–19.
8. J. Beeler,' Castles and strategy in Norman and early Angevin England', *Speculum* 31, 1956, p.588.
9. D. Renn, 'Chastell de Dynan: the first phases of Ludlow', in R. Avent and J. R. Kenyon (eds.) *Castles in Wales and the marches*, Cardiff, University of Wales Press, 1987, p.82.
10. P. R. Davis, *Castles of the Welsh princes*, Swansea, Christopher Davies Publishing, 1988, p.11.
11. M. W. Thompson, *The rise of the castle*, Cambridge, Cambridge University Press, 1991, p. 151.
12. J. Beeler, *Warfare in England 1066–1189*, Ithaca, Cornell University Press, 1966, p.284.
13. J. Beeler, *Warfare in England 1066–1189*, Ithaca, Cornell University Press, 1966, pp.289–93.
14. F. Suppe, *Military institutions on the Welsh marches*, Woodbridge, Boydell Press, 1994, p.45.
15. F. Suppe, *Military institutions on the Welsh marches*, Woodbridge, Boydell Press, 1994, pp.50–51.
16. *Brut y Tywysogion*, p.75.
17. *Brut y Tywysogion*, p.102.
18. *Brut y Tywysogion*, p.35.
19. D. J. C. King, *The castle in England and Wales*, London, Routledge, 1991, pp.134–35.
20. M. W. Thompson, *The rise of the castle*, Cambridge, Cambridge University Press, 1991, p.120.
21. M. Prestwich, *Edward I*, London, Methuen, 1988, p.214.
22. M. Prestwich, *Edward I*, London, Methuen, 1988, pp.218–19.
23. M. W. Thompson, *The rise of the castle*, Cambridge, Cambridge University Press, 1991, p.123.
24. M. Prestwich, *Edward I*, London, Methuen, 1988, pp.230–31.

Chapter 7
Change over time

Throughout this survey of Anglo-Welsh warfare, several references have been made suggesting that either one side or the other was adopting techniques and methods commonly used by their adversaries, or adapting their own tactics towards a given situation. To conclude this study these instances will be looked at in more detail.

The first occasion of a change in tactics bringing startling results was in the Anglo Saxon campaign of 1063–1064, as described in Chapter 2. The rebel Earl Aelfgar of Mercia was dead, and the crown could turn its whole attention toward subjugating his ally, Gruffudd ap Llywelyn of Gwynedd.[1] Although the sources for the Anglo-Saxon campaign argue over the exact dates, placing it from either the winter of 1062 until the middle of 1063, or 1063–1064, they agree on the sequence of events. The campaign opened at mid-winter, when Earl Harold of Wessex led a mounted raiding party from Gloucester to Gruffudd's fortress of Rhuddlan. Gruffudd himself escaped the assault but the town and his fleet, which lay at anchor, were put to the torch. This success was followed up the following year with a double assault on Wales. Earl Tostig of Northumbria, Harold's brother, led a land army while Harold himself commanded a sea-borne force from Bristol.

Harold had grasped the essence of Welsh battle tactics and altered his own accordingly, for now he defeated the Welsh on their own terrain with their own tactics. He used small companies of light troops who were highly mobile, and infiltrated the rugged terrain. Raids and ambushes were launched, rather than efforts to bring the Welsh to pitched battle, as this would be futile. The naval force enabled Harold to outflank Welsh positions and defeat them by being more mobile than they themselves were. The use of ships also allowed the Anglo-Saxons to patrol the Irish sea and cut off any Welsh efforts to recruit mercenaries from Dublin. The whole campaign was a stunning success. Wales was subjugated and Gruffudd ap Llywelyn killed, and King Edward was able to install puppet rulers in his place. Defeating the Welsh by using their own tactics against them was a strategy that the Normans would not properly exploit for over 200 years.[2]

Initial efforts by the Normans to deal with the Welsh left a great deal to be desired. Ralph of Mantes, earl of Hereford from 1051, did not grasp the intricacies of Welsh strategy as Harold would. He was perhaps unlucky in that he took over as a border earl at the time when Gruffudd ap Llywelyn's power was at its height, but his efforts to defend against Welsh raids were failures. Attempting to mount his Anglo-Saxon levies, who had no experience at cavalry fighting, and use them as Norman knights was a recipe for disaster as the defeat of 1055 would prove.[3]

The arrival of the Normans en-masse following 1066 changed the situation along the whole border at a stroke. The most obvious change was the construction of castles to secure the border, followed by aggressive thrusts into Wales, consolidated by more castles. The use of castles to hold down and dominate captured territory, though new in England and Wales, was standard Norman military practice, as was the use of heavy cavalry on the battlefield. Castles may soon have proven their worth in this border warfare, withstanding the Welsh counter offensives of the 1090s, but heavy cavalry were of less use. As stated in Chapter 3, knights had little value in rough terrain where the armoured shock which was their very essence could not be used. What was needed instead were bodies of light, mobile troops, as demonstrated by Harold in 1064.

From an early date the Normans did make efforts to rectify this situation. The castles of Earl Hugh of Chester and his cousin Robert of Rhuddlan in north Wales were garrisoned not by knights, but by companies of archers and light cavalry. Both types of soldier would be of more use against the Welsh than knights would, for the less heavily armed and armoured men would be better able to keep up with Welsh raiders in the broken terrain. Realising their superiority against the Welsh, other marcher lords began to raise companies of light horse and soon units such as the muntatores of Shropshire were to be found along the marches.[4] These soldiers were used as castle guards, border patrol units, and mounted infantry to rapidly respond to a Welsh raid, pursue the raiders and destroy them.

However, despite their very apparent advantages in Welsh warfare, light cavalry seem to be entirely absent from the armies of Edward I. Great care was taken to raise large numbers of knights, and the mechanisms for recruiting both them and the infantry were improved by Edward, but no mention is made of light cavalry. Edward was a gifted strategist and commander, and his failure to recognise the worth of light horse is difficult to understand. However it is likely that many of the mounted infantry raised were in fact light horse, or were able to operate as such in the field.

On the part of the Welsh, the most obvious strategy that they adopted from the Normans was the construction and use of castles. As this has been discussed in the previous chapter, it is not necessary to repeat the details here. However, how the Welsh garrisoned their castles is unclear, no evidence of a system of castleries and castle guard such as that used in England survives. There is evidence to show that the princes of Gwynedd did emplace free kindred groups at strategic locations within their lands, and these would doubtlessly act as the defence force of that area.[5] If a kindred group was emplaced at or near a castle site, then it can be assumed that they would act as its garrison. By the thirteenth century a system of military service for terms of three days had come into being, and there is evidence to suggest that, local and defensive in nature as it evidently was due to its contracted nature, this service became one of castle guard in Wales.[6]

Castles owned by the princes might have been garrisoned by members of his *teulu*, or it is possible that men of the *teulu* would serve as the core of a garrison, and act as the officers for a unit of freemen of the district, who would owe the prince an unlimited period of service per annum in any case.[7] The castellan of a prince's castle would of course be a trusted member of his retinue, and again it is quite possible that he would be a member of the teulu. If castles were indeed garrisoned in this way, then we can see the men of the teulu acting in a similar way to those of the familia regis of the king, trusted household warriors given the tasks of command and garrisoning of strategic fortifications.

The Welsh were to learn more about warfare from their Norman enemies than just the use of castles, as Brut y Tywysogyon shows in the entry for 1136. That year the Normans despatched a relief force to the besieged castle of Cardigan, invested by the forces of Gwynedd. The Welsh and Norman troops met in battle at Crug Mawr, when, according to the chronicle the Welsh army included, 'Two thousand mailed horsemen ready for battle.'[8] We can assume that the figure of 2,000 is a wildly inflated total for the number of cavalry, but that they had heavy horse and were prepared to face the Normans in pitched battle at this time is most worthy of note. This was not a common Welsh tactic, but it was nevertheless successful, the Normans were heavily defeated.

Further evidence is afforded of the use of heavy cavalry by the Welsh, proving that they were employing Norman tactics against them when circumstances were favourable to their use. Gerald of Wales, writing in 1188, stated that:' The Welsh have gradually learnt from the English and the Normans how to manage their weapons and to use horses in battle, for they have frequented the court and been sent to England as hostages.'[9] Gerald was never more than a grudging admirer of the Welsh, attributing their methods to cowardice rather than to tactical acumen, but he too saw how they learned from their enemies, to their own advantage.

In 1263 John de Grey wrote to Henry III from the vicinity of Hereford and Brecon, stating that Llywelyn ap Gruffudd was in the area with a substantial army which included within its ranks 180 barded horses, as well as an unspecified amount of light cavalry.[10] This figure of heavy horse is rather more believable than the 2,000 from the Brut y Tywysogyon, and is further proof of their use. Who these heavy cavalry were though is not so easy to discover. It is possible that they were members of the princes' *teulu*, trained to fight as knights. They may have been the princes' tenants in chief and their retinues, serving in the same manner as English lords. No records of Welshmen serving the prince as feudal knights exist, and who these men were remains questionable.

Throughout the thirteenth century royal armies in Wales came to use more and more locally recruited troops. The local knowledge of these men, usually recruited from south Wales and the Marches, and their unquestioned abilities as light troops at raiding and skirmishing were invaluable to royal armies operating in Wales. Welsh infantry became common in campaigns, especially towards the close of the century. At one point in 1277 Edward I had some 9,000 Welsh infantry employed in the Chester army alone. It was through the use of Welsh troops that the Welsh were to have their greatest impact upon the English art of war. The Welsh of the south, especially Gwent, introduced the Anglo-Normans to the use of the longbow. Even by 1282 the majority of the infantry, both English and Welsh, in Edward I's armies were archers, and that proportion continued to increase.[11] Welsh archers formed a major part of the armies Edward I led to Scotland, being present at the decisive battle of Falkirk, for example (where they in fact played little part).

'English military institutions were improved by borrowing from Welsh practice and modifications made to meet the challenges posed by the Welsh.'[12] This is undeniably true, as the use of longbowmen and light cavalry have clearly shown. A similar statement could equally be applied to the Welsh, for interaction with their enemies brought to their attention the use of castles, siegecraft and heavy cavalry. Therefore we can see in these specific instances the two sides imitating each other as they tried to gain the upper hand. In this way the Anglo-Welsh wars can be seen as a learning process for both countries, and the innovations that they made aided both in their defence. However the wars did more than create a kind of arms race; a new society was created along the March, neither wholly Welsh nor English. Alliances within and outside of the March brought the princes of Wales firmly into the orbit of European politics, and by the close of the thirteenth century had seen the birth of a fledgling Welsh national identity.

Ultimately the innovations of the English were coupled to the vastly superior resources of the crown, and forged into a war machine that when commanded by a strong monarch not diverted by internal problems, could not be matched by the Welsh. Just as the Welsh had learned of castles and knights from the Normans, so the English learned of tactical variation and the longbow. By the close of the thirteenth century, the English were not just using Welsh archers, but were beginning to adopt the longbow themselves. At Falkirk the best archers seem to have been companies from Derbyshire, Lancashire and Cheshire.[13] It was the longbow which was largely responsible for the tactical dispositions of English armies on the battlefield in the fourteenth century. For the victories which they achieved both in Scotland and in France. The English Crown had to thank the Welsh for excellent tuition, and for over 200 years of very hard lessons.

Notes

1. B. T. Hudson, 'The death of Gruffydd ap Llywelyn', *Welsh History Review* 15, 1990–1991, pp.331–350.
2. R. R. Davies, *The age of conquest. Wales 1063–1415*, Oxford, Oxford University Press, 1992, p.26.
3. *Brut y Tywysogion*, p.130.
4. F. Suppe, *Military institutions on the Welsh marches*, Woodbridge, Boydell Press, 1994, pp.63–87.
5. G. R. J. Jones, 'The defences of Gwynedd in the thirteenth century', *Transactions of the Caernarvonshire Historical Society* 30, 1969, p.41.
6. F. Suppe, *Military institutions on the Welsh marches*, Woodbridge, Boydell Press, 1994, pp.133–138.
7. D. Stephenson, *The governance of Gwynedd*, Cardiff, University of Wales Press, 1984, p.89.
8. *Brut y Tywysogion*, p.51.
9. L. Thorpe, (ed.) *Gerald of Wales. The journey through Wales/The description of Wales*, London, Penguin, 1978, p.267.
10. J. G. Edwards, (ed.) *Calendar of ancient correspondence concerning Wales*, Cardiff, University of Wales Press, 1935, pp.17–18.
11. M. Prestwich, *Armies and warfare in the middle ages. The English experience*, New Haven, Yale University Press, 1996, p.133.
12. F. Suppe, *Military institutions on the Welsh marches*, Woodbridge, Boydell Press, 1994, p.149.

13. M. Prestwich, *Armies and warfare in the middle ages. The English experience*, New Haven, Yale University Press, 1996, p.133.

Bibliography

Primary sources

Chibnall, M. (ed.) (1973) *Ordericus Vitalis. The Ecclesiastical History*, v4, Oxford: Oxford University Press.

Chibnall, M. (ed.) (1973) *Ordericus Vitalis. The Ecclesiastical History*, v5, Oxford: Oxford University Press.

Douglas, D. C. Tucker, S. I. and Whitelock, D. (eds) (1961) *The Anglo-Saxon Chronicle*, London: Eyre and Spottiswoode.

Douglas, D. C. (ed.) (1968) *English Historical Documents* v.1, London: Eyre and Spottiswoode.

Douglas, D. C. (ed.) (1968) *English Historical Documents* v.2, London: Eyre and Spottiswoode.

Edwards, J. G. (ed.) (1935) *Calendar of Ancient Correspondence concerning Wales*, Cardiff: University Of Wales Press.

Edwards, J. G. (ed.) (1940) *Littere Wallie*, Cardiff: University of Wales Press.

Fryde, E. B. (ed.) (1962) *Book of Prests of the Kings wardrobe for 1294–5*, Oxford: Oxford University Press.

Jones, A. (ed.) (1910) *The History of Gruffydd ap Cynan*, Manchester: Manchester University Press.

Jones, T. (ed.) (1952) *Brut y Tywysogion*. Peniarth ms. 20 version, Cardiff: University of Wales Press.

Laing, S. (ed.) (1951) *Snorri Sturluson. Heimskringla*, London: Everyman.

Matthews, T. (ed.) (1910) *Welsh Records in Paris*, Carmarthen: W. Spurrell and Son.

Thorpe, L. (ed.) (1978) *Gerald of Wales. The journey through Wales./The description of Wales*, London: Penguin.

Secondary sources

Abels, R. P. (1988) *Lordship and Military Obligation in Anglo-Saxon England*, London: British Museum Publications.

Avent, R. and Kenyon, J. R. (eds) (1987) *Castles in Wales and the Marches*, Cardiff: University of Wales Press.

Barlow, F. (1965) *William I and the Norman Conquest*, London: English Universities Press.

Barlow, F. (1970) *Edward the Confessor*, London: Eyre and Spottiswoode.

Beeler, J. (1956) 'Castles and strategy in Norman and Angevin England', *Speculum* 31.

Beeler, J. (1966) *Warfare in England*, Ithaca: Cornell University Press.

Smith, J. Beverley. (1982–83) 'Llywelyn ap Gruffydd and the March of Wales', *Brycheiniog* 20–21.

Carr, A. D. (1982) *Llywelyn ap Gruffydd*, Cardiff: University of Wales Press.

Carr, A. D. (1982) 'The last days of Gwynedd', *Transactions of the Caernarfonshire Historical Society*, v.43.

Carr, A. D. (1989) 'Anglo-Welsh relations, 1066–1282', in M. Jones, and M. Vale, (eds) *England and her Neighbours 1066–1453*, London: Hambledon Press.

Carr, A. D. (forthcoming) 'Teulu and penteulu', in T. M. Charles-Edwards and M. E. Owen, (eds.) *The King and the Court*.

Charles, B. G. (1934) *Old Norse relations with Wales*, Cardiff: University of Wales Press.

Contamine, P. (1984) *War in the Middle Ages*, Oxford: Blackwell.

Crouch, D. (1984–86) 'The slow death of kingship in Glamorgan, 1067–1158', *Morgannwg* 28–30.

Crouch, D. (ed.) (1992) *The Image of Aristocracy in Britain 1000–1300*, London: Routledge.

Davies, P. R. (1988) *Castles of the Welsh Princes*, Swansea: Christopher Davies.

Davies, R. R. (1979) 'Kings, lords and liberties in the March of Wales 1066–1072', *Transactions of the Royal Historical Society* 29.

Davies, R. R. (1985) 'Henry I and Wales', in H. Mayr-Harting and R. I. Moore (eds) *Studies in Medieval History Presented to R. H. C. Davies*, London: Hambledon Press.

Davies, R. R. (1992) *The Age of Conquest. Wales 1063–1415*, Oxford: Oxford University Press.

Davies, W. (1990) *Patterns of Power in Early Wales*, Oxford: Oxford University Press.

Griffiths, R. A. (1994) *Conquerors and Conquered in Medieval Wales*, Stroud: Alan Sutton Publishing.

Hawkes, S. C. (ed.) (1989) *Weapons and Warfare in Anglo-Saxon England*, Oxford: Oxbow Books.

Herbert, T. and Jones, G. E. (eds.) (1988) *Edward I and Wales*, Cardiff: University of Wales Press.

Hollister, C. W. (1962) *Anglo-Saxon Military Institutions on the eve of the Norman conquest*, Oxford: Oxford University Press.

Hollister, C. W. (1986) *Monarchy, Magnates and Institutions in the Anglo-Norman world*, London: Hambledon Press.

Hudson, B. T. (1990–91) 'The destruction of Gruffydd ap Llywelyn', *Welsh History Review* 15.

Jones, G. R. J. (1969) 'The defences of Gwynedd in the thirteeenth century', *Transactions of the Caernarfonshire Historical Society* 30.

King, D. J. C. and Spurgeon, C. J. (1965) 'The mottes in the vale of Montgomery', *Archaeologica Cambrensis* 114.

King, D. J. C. (1991) *The Castle in England and Wales*, London: Routledge.

Lewis, C. W. (1964) 'The Treaty of Woodstock, its background and significance', *Welsh History Review* 2.

Lloyd, J. E. (1899–1900) 'Wales and the coming of the Normans', Transactions of the *Honourable Society of Cymmrodorion*.

Lloyd, J. E. (1939) *A History of Wales from the Earliest Times to the Edwardian Conquest* v.2, London: Longmans.

Loyn, H. (1984) *The Governance of Anglo-Saxon England 500–1087*, London: Edward Arnold.

Loyn, H. (1994) *The Vikings in Britain*, Oxford: Blackwell.

Maund, K. L. (1991) *Ireland, Wales and England in the Eleventh Century*, Woodbridge: Boydell Press.

Moore, D. (1991) *The external relations of native Welsh rulers*, Unpublished thesis.

Morris, J. E. (1996) *The Welsh Wars of Edward I*, Stroud: Alan Sutton Publishing.

Nelson, L. H. (1966) *The Normans in South Wales 1070–1171*, Austin: University of Texas Press.

Nicolle, D. (1995) *Arthur and the Anglo-Saxon Wars*, London: Osprey.

Le Patourel, J. (1978) *The Norman Empire*, Oxford: Oxford University Press. Bibliography.

Powicke, F. M. (1947) *King Henry III and the Lord Edward* v.2, Oxford: Oxford University Press.

Powicke, F. M. (1953) *The Thirteenth Century 1216–1307*, Oxford: Oxford University Press.

Powicke, M. R. (1962) *Military Obligation in Medieval England*, Oxford: Oxford University Press.

Prestwich, M. (1972) *War, Politics and Finance under Edward I*, London: Faber and Faber.

Prestwich, M. (1988) *Edward I*, London: Methuen.

Prestwich, M. (1996) *Armies and Warfare in the Middle Ages. The English Experience*, New Haven: Yale University Press.

Pugh, T. B. (ed.) (1971) *Glamorgan County History* v.3, Cardiff: University of Wales Press.

Rees, W. (1966) *An Historical Atlas of Wales*, London: Faber and Faber.

Roderick, A. J. (1952) 'The feudal relation between the English crown and the Welsh princes', *History* 37.

Rowlands, I. W. (1980) 'The making of the March', *Proceedings of the Battle Conference on Anglo-Norman History* v.3, Woodbridge: Boydell Press.

Rotheroe, C. (1986) *The Scottish and Welsh Wars 1250–1400*, London: Osprey. Bibliography.

Stephenson, D. (1983) 'Llywelyn ap Gruffydd and the struggle for the principality of Wales 1258–1282', *Transactions of the Honourable Society of Cymmrodorion*.

Stephenson, D. (1984) *The Governance of Gwynedd*, Cardiff: University of Wales Press.

Stephenson, D. (1984) 'The politics of Powys Wenwynwyn in the thirteenth century', *Cambridge Medieval Celtic Studies* 7.

Strickland, M. (ed.) (1993) *Anglo-Norman Warfare*, Woodbridge: Boydell Press.

Suppe, F. C. (1994) *Military Institutions on the Welsh Marches*, Woodbridge: Boydell Press.

Taylor, A. J. (1985) *Studies in Castles and Castle Building*, London: Hambledon Press.

Thompson, M. W. (1991) *The Rise of the Castle*, Cambridge: Cambridge University Press.

Verbruggen, J. (1977) *The Art of Warfare in Western Europe during the Middle Ages*, Amsterdam: North-Holland Publishing.

Walker, D. (1977) *The Norman Conquerors*, Swansea: Christopher Davies Publishing.

Walker, R. F. (1972) 'Hubert de Burgh and Wales 1218–1232', *English Historical Review* 87.

Warner, P. (1977) *Famous Welsh Battles*, Glasgow: Fontana.

Warren, W. L. (1977) *Henry II*, London: Eyre Methuen.

Williams, G. A. (1963–64) 'The succession to Gwynedd 1238–47', *Bulletin of the Board of Celtic Studies* 20.

Appendix
Re-enactment Groups

The costume illustrations in this book were produced with the co-operation of three of the many re-enactment groups that now exist in Britain. The publishers would like to sincerely thank them their assistance and their knowledge of medieval Welsh warfare.

Mathrafal

'Mathrafal' is a re-enactment group based in north-east Wales and is a member of 'The Vikings', an international re-enactment society. Its members are dedicated to re-creating everyday life in the Early Middle Ages. Although primarily a Welsh group, 'Mathrafal' also has members who portray Irish and Hiberno-Norse characters from the period and, within the society, there are Norwegian, Swedish and Danish Vikings along with Anglo-Saxons. For further information please contact:'Mathrafal' 01978-845107 or mathrafal@aol.com; 'The Vikings' 01462-812208
or sandra.orchard@roche.com
or check out their websites — www.mathrafal.demon.co.uk
www.vikings.ndirect.co.uk

Samhain Welsh Medieval Society

Samhain Welsh Medieval Society depicts accurately the era from the times of Llywelyn Ap Gruffudd to Owain Glyndwr (1200 –1400). Everyday life and warfare is covered by our living history displays which range from strumming the harp to shooting the longbow, with some sword play in between! For further information contact: Michael Roberts, 13 Castle Street, Caergwrle, Flintshire, LL12 9WD

Regia Anglorum

Regia Anglorum is a group specifically interested in the re-creation of the life and times of the people who lived in and around the British Isles between the reigns of Alfred the Great and Richard the Lionheart. Founded in 1986, they have five full-scale ship replicas, a large living history encampment, perform major battle re-enactments and are currently engaged in the construction of a permanent site in Kent. For further information please contact: Regia Anglorum, 9 Durleigh Close, Headley Park, Bristol, BS13 7NQ or via the internet — www.regia.org

Royal Armouries
The Royal Armouries is the national museum of arms and armour. For information regarding opening times, rpices and special events write to Royal Armouries Museum, Armouries Drive, LEEDS, LS10 1LT or ring 0113-2201999.

Also available from
Bridge Books:

The Dissolution of Valle Crucis Abbey
Derrick Pratt

A fascinating and detailed academic study of the dissolution of the Cistercian abbey of Valle Crucis near Llangollen. Invaluable for any student of the Reformation in Wales.

'The Goode Mr Garbet of Wem'
Beryl M. Jones

The life and times of the Revd. Samuel Garbet, MA of Wem, Shropshire (1685–1756), cleric, schoolmaster and local historian. Using previously unknown primary sources, the author has pieced together the life of an 18th century provincial curate who was also the author of *The History of Wem*, one of the earliest local history studies of a small town. Illustrated

Dr Johnson and Mrs Thrale's Tour in North Wales, 1774
Adrian Bristow

Out of print since the beginning of the 10th century, the diaries of Dr Johnson and his friend Mrs Thrale provide an outsider's view of north Wales in the mid 18th century. Complete with a new introduction and extensive notes. Illustrated.